GREAT SPIRITUAL MASTERS

Their Answers to Six of Life's Questions

Also from John Farina
published by Paulist Press

AN AMERICAN EXPERIENCE OF GOD
The Spirituality of Isaac Hecker

HECKER STUDIES
Essays on the Thought of Isaac Hecker

ISAAC T. HECKER: THE DIARY
Sources of American Spirituality series

GREAT SPIRITUAL MASTERS

Their Answers to Six of Life's Questions

John Farina

PAULIST PRESS ◆ New York ◆ Mahwah, N.J.

Excerpts taken from: *Ignatius of Loyola: Spiritual Exercises and Selected Works*
© 1991 by Paulist Press; *Augustine of Hippo: Selected Writings* © 1984 by Paulist
Press; *Julian of Norwich: Showings* © 1978 by Paulist Press; *Gregory of Nyssa: The
Life of Moses* © 1978 by Paulist Press; *Bonaventure: The Soul's Journey into God, The
Tree of Life, The Life of St. Francis* © 1978 by Paulist Press, of the Classics of
Western Spirituality series, are used by permission of the publisher. *The Divine
Comedy of Dante Alighieri,* translated by Henry Wadsworth Longfellow,
Houghton, Mifflin and Company, 1895.

Book design by Theresa M. Sparacio

Cover design by Valerie Petro

Library of Congress Cataloging-in-Publication Data

Farina, John.
Great spiritual masters : their answers to six of life's questions / John Farina.
p.   cm.
Includes bibliographical references.
ISBN 0-8091-4080-2 (alk. paper)
1. Spiritual life—Catholic Church. 2. Christian saints. I. Title.
BX2350.3 .F37 2002
248.4′82—dc21
2002024181

Published by Paulist Press
997 Macarthur Boulevard
Mahwah, New Jersey 07430

www.paulistpress.com

Printed and bound in the
United States of America

Table of Contents

DEDICATION

To Lisa, io t'adoro

ACKNOWLEDGMENTS

I would like to thank the many people who made this book possible. First among them is my longtime friend, Roger Sorrentino, whose encouragement and literary talent are cherished. I would also like to thank Cheryl Hutchison for her expert help in preparing the manuscript. Special thanks to The Missionary Society of St. Paul the Apostle and the Paulist Press for carrying on the vision of Isaac Hecker, begun nearly a century and one-half ago. Father Lawrence Boadt, C.S.P., deserves appreciation for his deft editorial advice and his trust. I would also like to thank Father Kevin Lynch, C.S.P., for the opportunity he gave me many years ago to be associated with the Classics of Western Spirituality, which opened me to the wonder of presenting the spiritual wisdom of the past to our own age. Kathleen Doyle and Theresa Sparacio also deserve special thanks for their skill and good will.

Introduction

All of us face questions in our lives. Some are about matters of ultimate concern, what Clyde Crews calls "ultimate questions." Others are matters of curiosity. And still others, simply matters of indifference. In this book I have focused on six questions, five of which certainly could be characterized as ultimate questions; the sixth is, admittedly, a curiosity, but one with significant implications for our time. Chapter 1 deals with the question of self-mastery. Chapter 2 with the question of finding ultimate meaning by looking within ourselves. Chapter 3 with the question of how we speak about God and gender. Chapter 4 with the issue of how we improve ourselves. Chapter 5 with how we relate love, *eros,* and God in our lives. And Chapter 6 with the question of how we relate art and religion.

I have attempted to shed light on each of these questions by presenting the stories of those people from another age who have had extraordinary perceptions—divine seers, exemplars, religious geniuses, "saints." In my accounts of these saints, I have tried to reconnect their stories to our stories. After we have dug through the layers of hagiography, of mythology, of exaggeration, we find in the saints persons who felt the same sorrows, experienced the same fears, knew the same imperfections of being human. We find, as well, people who dreamed the same dreams about what their lives could be, about what made them happy, about what brought dignity and hope to their lives. As we share their humanity, we share their aspirations and their insights as well.

Each chapter contains a presentation of the question to be studied, a discussion of the insights of a particular saint, and a selection from the writings of that saint.

The ideas presented here are old and often forgotten, not new and undiscovered. Yet they are, in the final analysis, ideas about you and me—Western men and women living in the closing days of the Modern Age, a time, to borrow from Matthew Arnold, between two worlds, "one dead, the other powerless to be born." It is my conviction the saints' insights can speak freshly to us in a language rich with meaning and hope.

Chapter 1

GAINING SELF-MASTERY:
IGNATIUS OF LOYOLA

Sixteenth-century missionary, educator, and spiritual reformer, Ignatius of Loyola is one of the best-known figures in the history of Western spirituality. The movement he founded has had a major impact on education and evangelization worldwide. Through his writings he has been valued as a spiritual guide. His message has enduring value: All of creation exists for the greater glory of God. We are called to order our lives to that end through intellectual illumination that allows us to discern the moral value of our thoughts and deeds.

Controlling ourselves. It's a basic problem that we all face. Many wisdom traditions speak of its necessity. The Book of Proverbs says: "Better is he who controls himself than he who conquers a city." And again, "He that is without self-control is like a city that is broken down and without walls." The Buddha focused on the problem of wanting what we don't have as the root of human unhappiness. Until we freed ourselves from the endless succession of desires for things we did not have, he believed we would always be unhappy.

There is an old Shawnee folktale about a young man who wanted his father to make him a new bow and arrow. He asked his father nearly every day for this gift and thought about it constantly. His father grew weary of his pleading, for he had not planned to make him a bow for another year, when the boy had seen fifteen summers, the traditional time for the reception of the bow by young Shawnee braves. One day when the boy asked again, the father said: "Do you remember that young willow sapling by the stream that I showed you?"

"Yes, father."

"Bring it to me tomorrow, and I will make you your bow."

The boy was elated. He could hardly sleep, waiting for dawn. At first light he pulled on his moccasins and went out into the forest with an axe. He found the tree, still wet with the morning dew,

and began to hack at its base. The green wood seemed to absorb
the axe, which though sharp, was of little good. Growing impa-
tient, the boy bent the sapling and cracked it off. He ran back to his
father and proudly presented him with the tree.

Three days later, the bow was finished. His father gave it to
him and told him to go into the field and shoot. The boy was filled
with expectation as he drew back the bow, for he knew his father
made very fine bows. As he pulled back the string, he noticed it
was easier to pull than other bows he had shot. He then released
the first arrow at a target about forty feet away. To his horror he
saw the arrow drop lifelessly about ten feet short of its goal. He
tried a second arrow. Again it was slow and without force. A third,
a fourth, a fifth, all with the same result.

Dejected, he ran back to his father.

"Father, this bow is weak. It shoots very poorly."

"What do you expect? The wood it is made from is too
young. It needed another year to grow and strengthen."

Saddened, the young boy went off, holding the worthless
fruits of his lack of self-control.

Like that young brave, many of us must have what we want at
any price. Today addiction is a major health problem in America.
Addictions are classic cases of a lack of impulse control. Addicts
become fixated on certain behaviors and cannot seem to let go,
even though they know the harmful effects of their actions.
Whether it's a substance like tobacco, cocaine, alcohol, food, or
actions like gambling, viewing pornography, or the compulsive
repetition of everyday acts like hand washing, self-control is a
problem for many in today's world.

Even when actions do not rise to the level of addictions, we
often have trouble controlling ourselves. How many of us have
responded badly to perceived insults on the highway? "Road rage"
is described by some like psychologist Arnold Neremberg as a
mental disorder. That "disorder" is apparently widespread. The
National Highway Safety Administration estimated in 1997 that
two-thirds of the 41,000 persons killed in auto accidents that year

died as a result of road range. The killing of Bud Crihfield and his teenage daughter by their Aurora, Colorado, neighbor, Elsworth Walker, was a case of road rage at its worst. Walker fired four shots from a large caliber handgun into Crihfield's car, because he had parked in Walker's parking space.

Black male schoolchildren in Baltimore face terrible odds. Two-thirds won't graduate from high school. Fifty percent will be convicted of a felony. Baltimore's public schools have nearly buckled under the pressure. When asked what is most needed, teachers often say get the troublemakers out so that the others can learn.

Robert Embry of Baltimore's Abell Foundation heard that message and started sending troubled kids to rural boarding schools in Kenya. The Kenyan schools offered strong discipline, lots of adult supervision, and, with the nearest city, TV, and phone thirty miles away, freedom from the negative influence of the streets. Students like Brendon Harlee responded. Harlee completed the African program and returned to Baltimore a successful student and entered a first-class magnet school program. Harlee says, "I learned self-control" while in Kenya.

Like Harlee, Randy DeVaney has found that training in self-control is a key to his rehabilitation. DeVaney is an inmate at Four Mile Correctional Center, a prison near Colorado Springs, Colorado. He is part of a program started by Brian Hardin that teaches prisoners how to train wild horses. The program uses methods made popular in Robert Redford's movie *The Horse Whisperer.* Through persistent, gentle discipline, horses are trained to accept riders rather than "broken." Working with the horses teaches patience and discipline says Hardin, and the prisoners often incorporate those skills into their own efforts to fashion more positive lives when they leave jail.

Self-control is behind some of the problems young learners have with school, which we hear so much about. In the United States, a battle is raging between the friends and foes of Ritalin. Advocates such as Children and Adults with Attention Deficit

Disorder (CHADD) claim that a genuine health crisis exists. Attention Deficit Disorder (ADD) is a medical condition, which can be accurately diagnosed. Its symptoms include poor attention span, impulsiveness, and sometimes hyperactivity. Persons with ADD, it is claimed, have a hard time finishing an assignment, fidget often, forget things, and get distracted easily.

This condition is caused by an irregularity in brain function that results in too little activity in the area that inhibits impulsive behaviors. Ritalin is a methylphenidate that stimulates the central nervous system and fixes the ADD problem, according to CHADD and other advocates.

Opponents argue that Ritalin enhances the ability to concentrate in anyone, just as do cocaine and other Class II narcotics to which it is related, dexies and crystal meth. ADD is an over-diagnosed condition, with prescriptions up 700 percent since 1990. By drugging kids, foes of Ritalin claim, we are only masking the real issues, which often are nothing more complex than leaning self-control and discipline through the normal processes of maturation and education. Once again, self-control is the heart of the matter.

Faced with this, we are compelled to ask what we can do about it. Of course, even though the television infomercials and mountebanks assure us there is an easy cure, we all know better. Yet there are positive, helpful ways for us to improve ourselves by analyzing our actions to discern what motivates us. Few persons were more expert at that than Ignatius of Loyola. The method he developed for spiritual direction focused on gaining self-mastery through knowledge, effort, and grace. He wrote a whole book about it. The title in its long form says it all:

Spiritual Exercises
To gain mastery over one's self and to live a well-ordered life
not making life choices that take shape from disordered
    affections.

"Disordered affections": a sixteenth-century way of speaking about the things that bedevil us. Craving things. Letting things get out of balance. Bad choices, bad habits. We are buffeted by them; sometimes we are overwhelmed by them so that we are falling and do not know it. Other times, when we have walked with these treacherous friends over many miles and have put aside all our initial misgivings and begun to trust that maybe, despite what we know deep inside, it will all work out, they turn on us and rend us, leaving us to die on the wayside.

In either case, disordered affections can bend our lives so far out of line that getting back can take forever.

Order. It's a word we don't hear much about these days. It signifies harmonious arrangement and continuity among the parts of a whole. We perhaps are most familiar thinking about order in the commonwealth, civil order. Moral order is the type of order that we are least accustomed to hearing about. Moral order is an attribute of the healthy soul. Virtuous actions promote moral order; vices destroy it. As Plato argued in the *Republic,* a society that embodies the virtues in its political and social structures is a reflection of the virtue and order in the souls of its citizens.

Ignatius understood that decisions based on vices would inevitably distort our lives. He developed a series of exercises to help train a person to avoid falling into the trap of acting on those disordered desires. The *Spiritual Exercises* is more of a manual than anything else, a "how-to" book to help people make decisions about their lives. It sets out a method to look at one's self and discern which ideas, motives, or plans of action are ultimately healthful and which are not.

Ironically, following spiritual disciplines is just what those who end up in Twelve Step recovery programs do. Their lives contain all of the classical marks of religious experience. Their lifestyle embodies the ageless spiritual disciplines of self-denial, detachment, study, prayer, spiritual counsel, and fellowship with believers. For millions of people who would never have thought of themselves as religious, the Twelve Step world gives them just what their childhood religious training often lacked. Many attended Sunday school; they went to catechism, received the sacraments, and were initiated into the life of the church. But mostly they received a heady, abstract knowledge of their faith and were never able to internalize religious belief and make it their own in an adult, responsible way. Norms of conduct were presented in terms of what not to do: *Thou shalt not steal. Thou shalt not lie.*

Twelve Step programs invert that order. They place little emphasis on doctrine and a great deal on action. They model behaviors that are the goal of the recovery program. Little things are important: how you spend your spare time, who your friends are, how often you attend meetings, how closely you follow the daily routine.

Buddhism can have much the same emphasis on the methods of self-mastery. A Buddhist master teaching his students *zazen* does not begin with doctrinal instruction. He does not talk about the meaning of life or the nature of the universe. He does not recite the Fourfold Path or the Eight Noble Truths. Rather, he shows his students how to sit in the half-lotus position. He then shows them what to do with their hands, then how to breathe. Later he shows them how to stand and how to walk.

Ignatius understood this, and it is to his life and method that we now turn.

IGNATIUS'S LIFE AND TIMES

Ignatius was born a Basque in the Guipuzcoa region of northern Spain in 1491. His father was a liegeman of Ferdinand and Isabella, who at that time were consolidating their rule over the Iberian Peninsula. In that year, with the fall of Grenada, the Moslems were expelled from Spain. The following year the Genovese mariner Christoforo Colombo reached the Americas and began the great intercontinental exchange that would make Spain a world power.

Ignatius spent his young manhood as a courtier in the service of the king's treasurer, Don Juan Velazquez de Cuellar. He received a thorough grounding in the manners and customs of the Spanish nobility. He was a gentleman with a highly refined sense of honor, obligation, and loyalty. He was also a young man who enjoyed women, drink, parties, and fighting.

His love of adventure led him into battle against the French in the city of Pamplona in 1521. As he stood on the ramparts of the city, a cannonball shattered his leg, nearly killing him. A long and painful recuperation in Loyola followed, during which he was confined to bed. During the primitive surgery that doctors performed to try to repair his leg, he insisted that they saw off a protruding bone dislocated by the blast. With time he began to regain strength, but he was never to walk without a limp again.

During his confinement, he read Ludolph of Saxony's *Life of Christ* that challenged him to make his faith the center of his life. He also read lives of Augustine and St. Dominic, two men who centuries earlier had decided to radically imitate Christ and to create communities of men who would live together to challenge one another to lives of discipleship.

As he lay in his sickbed, he could sense that the world was in the midst of a profound change. In fact the epochal changes swirling about him were among the most far-reaching in the history of Western religion. The first has already been mentioned: the discovery of the New World. The effect of that discovery for Christianity was profound. The new continent presented a missionary challenge to Christians who had been charged by their Lord to "go and make disciples of all nations." Vast new lands populated by people who had never heard the Good News beckoned to hundreds of Franciscan, Jesuit, and Dominican missionaries across the Ocean Sea.

Equally significant was the religious turmoil within Europe. In 1517 an Augustinian monk and professor had nailed his Ninety-Five Theses on the cathedral door at Wittenberg and begun the debate that was soon to divide Western Christianity. By 1521, the year of Ignatius's conversion, the young man Luther was excommunicated, and the apocalyptic rending of Western Christianity began. The Reformation was a result not only of new ideas, but of new

quests for power among the feudal lords of Europe who, like
Spain's own Isabella and Ferdinand, were forging their kingdoms
into nation-states. Fueled by a desire for political and financial
independence from Rome, leaders like Frederick of Saxony
embraced the ideas of Luther enthusiastically. The reliance on the
individual's ability to interpret Scripture and to participate in the
priesthood of all believers made independence from foreign
church powers a viable option. While rulers like Francis I in France
and John III in Portugal battled for new dominions, Henry VIII in
1531 formed the Church of England in what was the most dra-
matic grab for power of the age.

Even though the south of Europe remained faithful to
Rome, the need for reform was widespread and openly acknowledged. Superstition, ignorance, and immorality were widespread.
Preaching by a parish priest was unheard of. Many priests did not
know the proper order for the Mass and other basic rituals. In
some regions, bishops were absent from their dioceses for years on
end. Illiteracy was common, with fewer than 5 percent of the pop-
ulation able to read. In 1545, Pope Paul III convened the Council
of Trent, which attempted to initiate a series of sweeping reforms
to respond to the low state of affairs within the church and to the
challenges of Protestant reformers.

Not only was the world around Ignatius changing but the
world within was changing as well. Lying in his sickbed day after
day without the distractions of the court to disturb him, he
became acutely aware of his inner states. He noticed what motivated him. What caused him to think positive thoughts? Which
thoughts were profitable in bringing about certain behaviors and
which were negative and debilitating? He spent hours thinking
about how he would win the heart of a certain noble lady he had
known, only to discover that it left him with an uneasy, gnawing
feeling inside. At other times he imagined himself following the
examples of a man like Francis of Assisi, and those thoughts gave
him hope and confidence.

He began writing to keep track of how he was feeling with the idea that he could achieve certain goals even though he was still unable to leave his bed. The conquest he had relished as a soldier he preserved, but in a transformed version. The battlefield was now within. The enemy was sin. It was to be ruthlessly pursued wherever it hid: locked inside old habits, disguised behind virtues, protected by good intentions, or boldly standing in the open. The weapons at his disposal were taken from the array of mental powers open to the individual. True to his time, he valued those powers and did not see humans as mere puppets of fate. They could exercise their memory, their emotions, their wills to make their lives better.

Ignatius slowly but steadily recovered. His time of sickness had changed him and filled him with a resolve to live as a courtier in the Court of the Most High God. He would be a knight of Christ. He would follow Christ and serve him and his church no matter what the cost to himself. Shortly after recuperating, he went to Montserrat in March of 1522 where—as was common for knights at the beginning of their service—he made an all-night vigil before the shrine of the Blessed Virgin Mary. As a courtier, he knew every knight required a lady. Every cause needed the inspiration of a beautiful woman if it were to stir the hearts of men. Mary would be his lady. It was not in any sense a unique choice. He was imbued with a culture based on a Christianity that was rich in devotions, symbols, and ritual. He never rebelled against it. He had sown his wild oats but never eaten at the table of another god. His conversion was to a life of radical action. He was becoming a knight to be sure, putting aside boyish ways and a life of fecklessness, but he had been a member of the court for his whole life.

After the Montserrat pilgrimage, he traveled to the nearby town of Manresa, where he was to remain for nearly a year. In that city he engaged in a rigorous asceticism. He would walk around in sackcloth—a far cry from the fineness of dress he had been accustomed to—and spend long hours in fasting and prayer. During this time he experienced a series of mystical illuminations that were to become the basis of much of his future thought and action. Those insights had three foci. First, they focused on the Trinity. He began to see the interaction of the three persons of the Godhead "in the form [of harmony] of three musical tones." Second, he obtained new insights into God as Creator. As one of his earliest friends wrote of him: "He seemed to see something white, from which some rays were coming, and God made light from this." Third, he received a new, clearer, intellectual vision that unified all of his previous knowledge. As he walked along the banks of the Cardoner River that runs through the town, "the eyes of his understanding began to be opened; not that he saw any vision, but he understood and learned many things, both spiritual and matters of scholarship, and this with so great an enlightenment that everything seemed new to him."

From the banks of the Cardoner, Ignatius went to Venice, bent on going to the Holy Land to proclaim the Gospel to the infidels. His courtly, militaristic background, no doubt, made him want to conquer the age-old enemy of Christians now with new spiritual weapons, not merely with his sword and dagger. Arriving in the Holy Land in the fall of 1523, his stay in Jerusalem was brief. He was turned away by the Franciscans, who told him that the kind of preaching he wanted to do was not allowed in the city and that if he did not leave the city, they could not guarantee his safety. Sobered but not defeated, he returned to Europe and decided to go to university and complete his education to better prepare himself for mission work.

As a man of thirty-three, middle-aged by standards of his day, he enrolled in the University of Paris. He became a member of the College of Sante-Barbe, where he studied the scholastic philosophy of Thomas Aquinas, Albertus Magnus, Duns Scotus, and Peter Lombard. Thomas's comprehensive view of the procession of creatures from God and their return to him in Christ greatly impressed Ignatius and became the basis for the opening part of the *Exercises,* called the Principle and Foundation. He soon gathered around himself a group of like-minded younger men who wished to combine a radical Christian discipleship with their studies. They called themselves simply the companions. It was the beginning of what would be called the Society of Jesus.

In 1537, after completing his studies, Ignatius was ordained to the priesthood. The next year he and the companions offered themselves to the service of Pope Paul III to work as missionaries in the Holy Land. The pope urged them to consider working within the church in Europe and suggested that they form a religious order. A preliminary rule was drawn up and later approved in 1540. Ignatius was elected the first superior general of the new group, a post that he retained for the remaining fifteen years of his life. The Society experienced rapid growth throughout Europe. They founded schools, conducted missions, wrote catechisms and works of apologetics. By the time of Ignatius's death, there were approximately a thousand members living in twelve provinces in Portugal, Spain, India, Italy, Brazil, France, and Germany.

THE *SPIRITUAL EXERCISES*

The Outline

The *Spiritual Exercises* is the best known and most influential of Ignatius's writings. Begun in 1522, it was not published until twenty-six years later, in 1548. Lying in his sickbed after his last military campaign, Ignatius became more aware of his own interiority. With his later university study, he developed that awareness more acutely. Fundamental to the spiritual life is this shift from being outer-directed to becoming sensitive to the movements of one's own spirit: one's thoughts, feelings, desires. Beyond that, it involves becoming sensitive to our own bodies: our breathing, our appetites, our sleep, our attention. After nearly dying, how could he find the courage to get out of his bed and face life with a lame leg, no longer a youth but a man who had realized that much of what he had been doing for nearly half his life had been less than worthwhile? Only by taking charge of his own wants, reason, and imagination and directing them toward the will of God. That is what the *Spiritual Exercises* attempts to do.

To be sure, in his time, there was a large body of literature of spiritual devotion. Often it took the form of instructions on the spiritual life written by a master to his students. Works like the *Cloud of Unknowing* and John Climacus's *Ladder of Divine Ascent* could be placed alongside others by Thomas à Kempis and Bernard of Clairvaux. There were also many prophetic, visionary texts whose main purpose was to comment on the moral turpitude of the times and offer a glimpse of God's impending judgment. Hildegard of Bingen's *Scivias* or Joichim di Fiore's writings were such works.

Ignatius had a more practical and personal approach in mind. He wanted to make available for his companions and those that might follow later, the method he had found helpful in his own life and in the lives of his close associates. With that purpose in mind, he produced a manual to guide those going through the *Exercises* under the guidance of a director. It was designed to be used by those who wanted a more intense spiritual life and needed particular methods to help them. It contains methods of prayer, meditation, and directives for making rightly ordered choices or "elections." It is composed of twenty introductory explanations, some written for the director, others for the exercitant. It then states the goal of the exercises and the main principle or foundation on which they are constructed. What follows are four groups of meditations, divided into weeks.

The First Week of exercises aims at purging the soul of obstacles that keep one from God. It presents a history of human sinfulness, beginning with the rebellion of the angels and moving through the sin of Adam and Eve. It then focuses the attention of the exercitant on her own particular sins and the consequences of those sins.

The Second Week emphasizes the development of virtues that help a person live a Christlike life. The opening meditation presents Christ as the leader of an army arrayed for battle against evil. Satan is the wicked tyrant whose terrified followers slavishly do his bidding in the service of evil. The next three days of the week are given to devotions on the incarnation of Christ, the nativity, and hidden life of Christ. For the next six days, two series of exercises run at the same time: meditations on various events from Christ's public ministry; and principles applied to the times, suitable for making a sound decision and to two methods of making such a decision about an important matter.

The Third and Fourth Weeks present exercises aimed at bringing about union with Christ. During the Third Week emphasis is placed on identifying with the sufferings of Christ, and the exercitant is presented with a series of detailed meditations on the passion of Christ. During the Fourth Week the emphasis shifts to the experience of the joy of the risen Christ. As one has known Christ in his death, so one now is invited to know him in his resurrection and to draw close to him in a loving, intimate manner. The entire span of Christ's life is thus presented with the person living it over the weeks, drawing close, feeling the pains, knowing the joys and the newfound power of the resurrection.

The Goal

The above process reflects the single goal articulated in the subtitle to the *Spiritual Exercises:* "to gain self mastery and to order one's life." Furthermore, because Ignatius realized how important it was to make the right decisions in life, he wanted to avoid the catastrophe of making a major decision on the basis of a disordered affection. He had done so when he chose to be a courtier, or so he thought. Again he had done so when he went into battle to fight for glory and riches. Finally in midlife he learned to pay very close attention to what was going on inside himself and fit that carefully into the external events around him. He knew the importance of making right choices in part because he spent so much time working with young men who were at university, beginning their careers. They naturally thought of the future and faced many significant

choices that would shape their lives. They felt the urgency of the
choice, although often did not realize that they might be choosing
for the wrong motives. Often they did not begin to have the awareness of their own inner processes to enable them to analyze their
motives clearly.

Ignatius presented a remarkably detailed way to analyze one's
own decision-making process. In his awareness of the cognitional
process itself, Ignatius was a thoroughly modern thinker, and it is
no surprise that Bernard Lonergan, a twentieth-century Canadian
theologian whose ideas on the cognitional process are among the
most original to date, was himself a Jesuit.

The Method

The method consists mainly in exercising all of our powers to
get rid of disordered affections and seek God's will in fulfilling the
main purpose of our lives. "Exercising," with its clear allusion to
physical exercise, is just what Ignatius intends. Just as we must exercise our physical bodies to attain mastery over them and be healthy,
so too must we exercise our spiritual powers.

For Ignatius, our powers were memory, intellect, and will.
Here the three-part division of the person stretching back to
Augustine is evident. Ignatius accepts it largely intact and simply
makes use of it in his method. Because our contemporary sense
of memory, intellect, and will is somewhat different, the three
powers require some explanation. This is especially true when it
comes to the first of these: memory. Memory, for Ignatius, has a
connotation that is significantly broader than our current understanding. Memory means not only the power to reconstruct the
past in our minds, but the faculty of imagination. Throughout the
Exercises we are called to use our memory to imagine the details
of a bygone place and to imagine ourselves in that place, talking
to the people, seeing what they see, smelling what they smell,
feeling what they feel.

Intellect is the rational power by which the mind orders, analyzes, and deduces truths about the things it perceives through the five senses. It is also the ability to understand and to obtain insight.

Will is the volitional power of the soul that orders us to action. By means of it the process of perception, reflection, analysis, and judgment results in outward behavior.

Today people often think of the role of the intellect and the emotions when considering motivations for human behavior. Ignatius's word for emotions is "affections," and we have already seen that he was most concerned with making sure that disordered affections did not influence our actions. Clearly, in his view, the affections were controlled by the intellect and the will. As we clearly reason about a particular choice and will to perform the alternative that our intellect has commended, our affections are brought into line. Self-mastery involved self-understanding: "What fills the soul is understanding profoundly."

A look at one of the most famous meditations in the *Exercises* clarifies the ways in which the memory, intellect, and will work together in the Ignatian method to bring one more deeply into contact with spiritual truths. The Fourth Day of the Second Week presents a meditation on two standards: "the one of Christ, our supreme commander and Lord; the other of Lucifer, the moral enemy of our human nature." It follows the usual pattern for meditations in the *Exercises,* beginning with the Preparatory Prayer that is a prayer in which the exercitant asks God for whatever it is that he wants to get out of the meditation. In the words of the *Exercises,* one asks for "the grace that all my intentions, actions, and operations [those powers of the soul that depend directly on sensory perception] may be ordered purely to the service and praise of his Divine Majesty." Here the will is primarily engaged, directing the attention of the soul onto the topic at hand for the good purpose that the intellect has determined is appropriate.

Next come the Preludes, a series of imaginative exercises that call upon the faculty of memory. They consist in imagining the physical place in which an event or scene is taking place. Great detail is to be given to every element of the scene, its shape, color, and texture. Every sense is to be employed. What would you smell? What would you feel both through your senses and in your heart? What would you taste? In our age, in which the imagination has become so impoverished by constant reliance on external, electronic stimuli that do our imagining for us, it is hard to conceive of a person concentrating so profoundly on a mental image so as to actually smell, touch, and taste it. This is virtual reality, sixteenth-century style, in which prayer is a gateway to a new world, every bit as dazzling as Hollywood is to people today.

In the Second Prelude to this meditation, we are asked to imagine a great plain in the region of Jerusalem, where the supreme commander of the good people is Christ; and another plain near Babylon, where the leader of the enemy is Lucifer. We are asked to see Satan dealing harshly with his lieutenants, ordering them to spare no efforts to snare and destroy people by tempting them with riches, vainglory, and pride. Christ, on the other hand, sends out his witnesses to aid all persons, attracting them by good deeds and humility.

The Preludes are followed by one or more colloquies with the persons present in the meditation. So vivid is the scene to the imagination, so riveting for all the senses, that we are called upon now to actually converse with the characters; to stop the action and have a chat with those involved. In this meditation, the first colloquy is to be with the Blessed Virgin, to ask her how we might best approach her Son so that we might serve under his standard. The second colloquy is with the Son himself, in which we ask him for the grace to follow him, though it involved great hardship and poverty. The third colloquy is with the Father, that he may also grant us that grace.

In addition to the methods discussed above, one of the most frequently used deals with the temptation to respond to something in a disordered way. Should an exercitant find herself leaning in that direction she should "come over to the opposite of the thing." For example, if she is inclined to take a job because it is prestigious and well paying, she should pray for a job that is low paying and not highly regarded. In that way she will most effectively conquer that disordered affection that would seek pride and self-gain before the will of God.

Another frequently used method is the discernment of spirits. We have seen it already in the careful analysis of thoughts and behaviors characteristic of the entire *Exercises.* The only additions are the specific suggestions Ignatius gave for discerning the difference between the influence of the evil spirit and the good spirit. One was to follow a given thought carefully to its end—Ignatius called it searching for the serpent's tail. If that end were evil, the initial motivation or some step in the train of thought was flawed.

PRINCIPLE AND FOUNDATION

Underlying all these methods is what Ignatius called the Principle and Foundation, presented in the beginning of Week One:

> Human beings are created to praise, reverence, and serve God our Lord, and by means of this to save their souls.
>
> The other things on the face of the earth are created for human beings, to help them in working toward the end for which they are created.
>
> From this it follows that I should use these things to the extent that they help me toward my end, and rid myself of them to the extent that they hinder me.
>
> To do this, I must make myself indifferent to all created things, in regard to everything which is left to my freedom of will and is not forbidden....
>
> I ought to desire and elect only the thing that is more conducive to the end for which I am created (23).

There are three points to notice about this. First it is a statement about the purpose of human existence. Ignatius is in no way innovative in his insistence that the goal of human life is to praise

God. Nor is he unusual in insisting that is the way for human beings to save their souls. What was so fundamental to Ignatius and to any of his readers be they Jews, Moslems, or Christians is, however, equally foreign to many inhabitants of the postmodern West. We have purpose. It is not something we create. It does not depend on our opinions or our ethnic backgrounds. It is universal, definite, and unchanging.

Although not unique, Ignatius's insistence on this point must be underscored as a hallmark of his message. Everything, he tells us, must be seen as existing for the greater glory of God. All of our choices, all of our actions must be measured in the light of this great purpose.

Can we in any way begin to bridge the gap between such an understanding and our world, in which the individual defines his own realities, often reigns supreme in choosing his own destiny, and believes that relativity and change are the only universals?

Probably not. It misses the point even to suggest that this gap could be bridged by Ignatius's system of avoiding the choices that lead to personal failures. If we simply try to take his method without his premises, we are left with an odd duck, to say the least.

The question of the ultimate purpose of life leads us to the issue of truth. If we take even the first step into Ignatius's world, we must confront this. He believes that there is Truth. God is Truth. We can know what is true, what is good, and what is beautiful by knowing God. Furthermore, he believes that we have the choice of ordering our lives around what really is—that is, around the truth that is God and God's will—or around what may seem to be good, but may be in fact evil: a disordered affection.

If I am in an AA program, I must certainly face this. I must not only accept the notion that there is a "higher power" but also that an AA program can reveal it. Not just a truth, or a truth that might be true for somebody else in the program but not for me, but true. A purely pragmatic approach would say that it does not matter whether what I believe is true, just whether it works for me. But unless I believe it to be true, I cannot let it change me—and change is precisely what I need. As long as I rely on my own judgments exclusively, I remain where I am. I continue to think that I am all right, even though the rest of the world does not.

There is simply no way around Ignatius's principle axiom: We have a purpose.

The second point about the Principle and Foundation is its view of the rest of creation. People for the Ethical Treatment of Animals would not like Ignatius's Aristotelian notion of the hierarchy of creation. "All things on the face of the earth are created for humans," he says starkly. Here, however, there is a way to interpret this that makes more sense to those who see stewardship of the earth and belief in a Creator as complementary. Ignatius no doubt had little sense of human beings as caretakers of God's creation. He was not a protoenvironmentalist, as was St. Francis of Assisi. Rather he was concerned with human choices. What may a person do? Are there things that by their very nature as created things are prohibited? Ignatius's answer, when seen in the light of his times, is an optimistic one of the goodness of creation and of human nature. All things may be used by men and women. In one sense, whether we choose gold, silver, or tin is a matter of indifference. There is nothing in the nature of those created things that makes them good or bad choices. What makes them such is the moral disposition we bring to the act of using them. If, on the one hand, we are greedy for gold because it is highly valued by people, then our use of gold will be flawed morally. If, on the other, we are truly willing to use whatever it is that God wills for us in a given situation, then there is no reason why we cannot use gold. In fact, if we follow Ignatius in his assertion that the greater glory of God is the purpose of all creation, then we can use the things of the world in a way that is in harmony with all of creation and not in rebellion against it by serving the lusts of the individual.

That does not rule out that there are some actions—as distinguished from creatures—that are intrinsically evil. Ignatius would not say that we may do anything, as long as our motives are pure. Certain actions may, by their very nature, always be morally wrong.

Yet the things of the earth, as creatures of God, are all able to bring glory to God.

Choosing what is, in the world's eyes, less valuable, more humble, less wanted, may not in a given instance be the will of God. We cannot assume that it is. We cannot assume that God wants us to have the tin cup instead of the gold one, for example, simply because we should be humble and eschew greed. Again the comparison with Francis is apt, because for him, there was a necessary predisposition for the humble, the lowly, the poor elements of creation.

The spiritually minded person might still prefer the lowly thing over the valued thing, mainly to train herself in indifference. By indifference, Ignatius did not mean careless, mindless indecision. His response to creation was not: "whatever." Indifference is a disciplined ability to refrain from only wanting what one's own desires dictate without reference to a larger reality, which Ignatius called "the will of God." It is an ability to hold oneself like a ship following a compass—steady, not tilting in one direction or the other.

This is an old idea, one that Christianity probably got from Greek thought. Aristotle, in the *Nicomachean Ethics,* IV, 1, describes the high-minded person as one who has a moderate attitude toward wealth, power, and every manner of good or bad luck that may befall him. He is not overjoyed when his luck is good, nor crushed when he loses. St. Paul, who grew up in Asia Minor and absorbed the Hellenistic philosophy that was the cultural underpinning of Mediterranean civilization of the first century, spoke of this *apatheia* when he said in his Letter to the Philippians, "I know how to be content in whatever situation I find myself. I know how to be hungry and I know how to be full. I know how to enjoy abundance, and I know how to suffer need…" (4:11–12).

To hold oneself on the compass course, however, requires training in how to "come to the opposite of the thing" until one's will is truly in the middle. So one who naturally is inclined to riches would have to prefer poverty. But, just as surely—and often more difficult for the scrupulous souls interested in religion—one who desires poverty would have to prefer riches.

THE WILL OF GOD

The concept of the will of God plays a crucial role in the *Spiritual Exercises.* It functions as a sign of the sum of reality, the expression of the really real that each individual must confront in making a decision.

We have already discussed the problem of whether or not this notion can be accepted or denied by one wishing to follow Ignatius's method. Without acceptance, the entire process is meaningless. But there is another question, equally important and more difficult to resolve. We might accept the idea that all things must work for the greater glory of God. It is another thing, however, to believe that God has a specific will for a particular situation. Can we know what that will is? Can we know what the will of God is for us in choosing our state in life, for example? Can we really know that God wants us to be married or to be single, to become a lawyer, to live in Chicago?

Ignatius answered yes to all of these. His method asks us to focus our attention on the choice before us; rid ourselves of the influence of disordered affections so that we are truly indifferent to the alternatives; beg God to inspire our wills and our intellects; consider the pros and cons and see to which side our reason inclines us, and finally to bring that decision before God in prayer. If we experience continued peace and tranquility about a choice, we can be sure it is God's will.

Should we need further assistance in reaching a decision we can try imagining a stranger in our situation. What would we counsel her to do? Or we might ask what other method for making the decision we could use, and see if it agrees with our intellect and yields the same peace of mind. Finally, we might imagine ourselves before the judgment seat of Christ and see how we would explain our decision before the Ruler of the universe.

There is another essential ingredient to this process. As noted, the *Exercises* were not intended to be performed alone or simply read as a self-help book. They were to be lived for a prolonged period, usually one month, under the supervision of a mentor, a wisdom figure experienced in guiding souls toward good choices. Ignatius was a Spanish Catholic who thought little of the idea that the Scriptures alone, without the guidance of the community, would yield sufficient spiritual light to an individual. Although the structure of *Exercises* centers largely around meditation on the Gospels, it is not by that fact alone that these processes are able to lead people to a knowledge of God's will. Constant interaction between the exercitant and the director was expected. The individual making the *Exercises,* to be sure, was the one who had to take the initiative. The director was only to help the process that was taking place. But without the focus and accountability brought by the presence of the director, the exercitant would be left at the mercy of myriad diversions and pitfalls.

At another point the distance between Ignatius and many of us also becomes apparent. In our culture of individuals being autonomous is a virtue, and being free the greatest virtue. We give up that independence reluctantly and find it easier to do what we want and move on if those around us try to stop us. Whether we think of ourselves as religious or not makes little difference, because there are plenty of private forms of spirituality available to give our choices a pious odor. So a woman leaves her husband, whom she loved like she had never loved another, because she prefers freedom to responsibility. A son leaves his parents because he wants to be out on his own. And a retired couple leaves their community of seventy years behind to move to Florida because that is what they have been working toward for forty years. Alone. We stand alone and we want God to stand there with us, telling us that our private worlds are secure, our decisions good, our lives worthwhile. But often God is not able to find us, for in our solitude we have become invisible— invisible to those who love us, invisible to our true selves, and even invisible to God, who, as Ignatius reminds us, dwells in the community of being.

BIBLIOGRAPHY

Bangert, William V. A *History of the Society of Jesus.* St. Louis: Institute of Jesuit Resources, 1986.

De Nicolas, Antonio T., *Powers of Imagining: Ignatius de Loyola.* Albany: Suny Press, 1986.

Egan, Harvey D. *The Spiritual Exercises and the Ignatian Mystical Method.* St. Louis: Institute of Jesuit Resources, 1976.

Ganss, George E., ed. *Ignatius of Loyola: Spiritual Exercises and Selected Works.* The Classics of Western Spirituality. New York/Mahwah, N.J.: Paulist Press, 1991.

Tetlow, Joseph. *Ignatius Loyola: Spiritual Exercises.* New York: Crossroad Publishing Company, 1992.

The Spiritual Exercises[1]

IHS
Introductory Explanations To Gain Some Understanding of the Spiritual Exercises Which Follow, and To Aid Both the One Who Gives Them and the One Who Receives Them.

[1] *The First Explanation.* By the term Spiritual Exercises we mean every method of examination of conscience, meditation, contemplation, vocal or mental prayer, and other spiritual activities, such as will be mentioned later. For, just as taking a walk, traveling on foot, and running are physical exercises, so is the name of spiritual exercises given to any means of preparing and disposing our soul to rid itself of all its disordered affections and then, after their removal, of seeking and finding God's will in the ordering of our life for the salvation of our soul.

[2] *The Second.* The person who gives to another the method and procedure for meditating or contemplating should accurately narrate the history contained in the contemplation or meditation, going over the points with only a brief or summary explanation. For in this way the person who is contemplating, by taking this history as the authentic foundation, and by going over it and reasoning about it for oneself, can thus discover something that will bring better understanding or a more personalized concept of the history—either through one's own reasoning or to the extent that the understanding is

---

1. *Ignatius of Loyola: Spiritual Exercises and Selected Works,* ed. George E. Ganss, the Classics of Western Spirituality (New York/Mahwah, N.J.: Paulist Press, 1991).

enlightened by God's grace. This brings more spiritual relish and spiritual fruit than if the one giving the Exercises had lengthily explained and amplified the meaning of the history. For, what fills and satisfies the soul consists, not in knowing much, but in our understanding the realities profoundly and in savoring them interiorly.

[3]   *The Third*. In all the following Spiritual Exercises we use the acts of the intellect in reasoning and of the will in eliciting acts of the affections. In regard to the affective acts which spring from the will we should note that when we are conversing with God our Lord or his saints vocally or mentally, greater reverence is demanded of us than when we are using the intellect to understand.

[4]   *The Fourth*. Four Weeks are taken for the following Exercises, corresponding to the four parts into which they are divided. That is, the First Week is devoted to the consideration and contemplation of sins; the Second, to the life of Christ our Lord up to and including Palm Sunday; the Third, to the Passion of Christ our Lord; and the Fourth, the Resurrection and Ascension. To this week are appended the Three Methods of Praying. However, this does not mean that each week must necessarily consist of seven or eight days. For during the First Week some persons happen to be slower in finding what they are seeking, that is, contrition, sorrow, and tears for their sins. Similarly, some persons work more diligently than others, and are more pushed back and forth and probed by different spirits. In some cases, therefore, the week needs to be shortened, and in others lengthened. This holds as well for all the following weeks, while the retreatant is seeking for what corresponds to their subject matter. But the Exercises ought to be completed in thirty days, more or less.

[5]   *The Fifth*. The persons who receive the Exercises will benefit greatly by entering upon them with great spirit and generosity

toward their Creator and Lord, and by offering all their desires and freedom to him so that his Divine Majesty can make use of their persons and of all they possess in whatsoever way is according to his most holy will.

[6]   *The Sixth.* When the one giving the Exercises notices that the person making them is not experiencing any spiritual motions in his or her soul, such as consolations or desolations, or is not being moved one way or another by different spirits, the director should question the exercitant much about the Exercises: Whether the exercitant is making them at the appointed times, how they are being made, and whether the Additional Directives are being diligently observed. The director should ask about each of these items in particular. Consolation and desolation are treated in [316–324], the Additional Directives in [73–90].

[7]   *The Seventh.* When the giver of the Exercises sees that the recipient is experiencing desolation and temptation, he or she should not treat the retreatant severely or harshly, but gently and kindly. The director should encourage and strengthen the exercitant for the future, unmask the deceptive tactics of the enemy of our human nature, and help the retreatant to prepare and dispose himself or herself for the consolation which will come.

[8]   *The Eighth.* According to the need perceived in the recipient with respect to the desolations and deceptive tactics of the enemy, and also the consolations, the giver of the Exercises may explain to the retreatant the rules of the First and Second Weeks for recognizing the different kinds of spirits, in [313–327 and 328–336].

[9]   *The Ninth.* This point should be noticed. When an exercitant spiritually inexperienced is going through the First Week of the Exercises he or she may be tempted grossly and openly,

for example, by being shown obstacles to going forward in the service of God our Lord, in the form of hardships, shame, fear about worldly honor, and the like. In such a case the one giving the Exercises should not explain to this retreatant the rules on different kinds of spirits for the Second Week. For to the same extent that the rules of the First Week will help him or her, those of the Second Week will be harmful. They are too subtle and advanced for such a one to understand.

[10]   *The Tenth.* When the one giving the Exercises perceives that the recipient is being assailed and tempted under the appearance of good, the proper time has come to explain to the retreatant the rules of the Second Week mentioned just above. For ordinarily the enemy of human nature tempts under the appearance of good more often when a person is performing the Exercises in the illuminative life, which corresponds to the Exercises of the Second Week, than in the purgative life, which corresponds to those of the First Week.

[11]   *The Eleventh.* It is helpful for a person receiving the Exercises of the First Week to know nothing about what is to be done in the Second, but to work diligently during the First Week at obtaining what he or she is seeking, just as if there were no anticipation of finding anything good in the Second.

[12]   *The Twelfth.* The one giving the Exercises should insist strongly with the person receiving them that he or she should remain for a full hour in each of the five Exercises or contemplations which will be made each day; and further, that the recipient should make sure always to have the satisfaction of knowing that a full hour was spent on the exercise—indeed, more rather than less. For the enemy usually exerts special efforts to get a person to shorten the hour of contemplation, mediation, or prayer.

[13]   *The Thirteenth.* This too should be noted. In time of consolation it is easy and scarcely taxing to remain in contemplation for a full hour, but during desolation it is very hard to
fill out the time. Hence, to act against the desolation and
overcome the temptations, the exercitant ought to remain
always a little longer than the full hour, and in this way
become accustomed not merely to resist the enemy but
even to defeat him.

[14]   *The Fourteenth.* If the one giving the Exercises sees that the
exercitant is proceeding with consolation and great fervor, he
or she should warn the person not to make some promise or
vow which is unconsidered or hasty. The more unstable the
director sees the exercitant to be, the more earnest should be
the forewarning and caution. For although it is altogether
right for someone to advise another to enter religious life,
which entails the taking of vows of obedience, poverty, and
chastity; and although a good work done under a vow is more
meritorious than one done without it; still one ought to
bestow much thought on the circumstances and character of
each person, and on the helps or hindrances one is likely to
meet with in carrying out what one wishes to promise.

[15]   *The Fifteenth.* The one giving the Exercises should not urge
the one receiving them toward poverty or any other promise more than toward their opposites, or to one state or way
of life more than to another. Outside the Exercises it is lawful and meritorious for us to counsel those who are probably suitable for it to choose continence, virginity, religious
life, and all forms of evangelical perfection. But during these
Spiritual Exercises when a person is seeking God's will, it is
more appropriate and far better that the Creator and Lord
himself should communicate himself to the devout soul,
embracing it with love, inciting it to praise of himself, and
disposing it for the way which will most enable the soul to

serve him in the future. Accordingly, the one giving the exercises ought not to lean or incline in either direction but rather, while standing by like the pointer of a scale in equilibrium, to allow the Creator to deal immediately with the creature and the creature with its Creator and Lord.

[16]   *The Sixteenth.* For this purpose—namely, that the Creator and Lord may with greater certainty be the one working in this creature—if by chance the exercitant feels an affection or inclination to something in a disordered way, it is profitable for that person to strive with all possible effort to come over to the opposite of that to which he or she is wrongly attached. Thus, if someone is inclined to pursue and hold on to an office or benefice not for the honor and glory of God our Lord or for the spiritual welfare of souls, but rather for one's own temporal advantages and interests, one should try to bring oneself to desire the opposite. One should make earnest prayers and other spiritual exercises and ask God our Lord for the contrary; that is, to have no desire for this office or benefice or anything else unless his Divine Majesty has put proper order into those desires, and has by this means so changed one's earlier attachment that one's motive in desiring or holding on to one thing rather than another will now be only the service, honor, and glory of his Divine Majesty.

[17]   *The Seventeenth.* Although the one giving the Exercises should not endeavor to ask about or know the personal thoughts of sins of the exercitant, it is very advantageous for the director to be faithfully informed about the various agitations and thoughts which the different spirits stir up in the retreatant. For then, in accordance with the person's greater or lesser progress, the director will be able to communicate spiritual exercises adapted to the needs of the person who is agitated in this way.

[18]   *The Eighteenth*. The Spiritual Exercises should be adapted to the disposition of the persons who desire to make them, that is, to their age, education, and ability. In this way someone who is uneducated or has a weak constitution will not be given things he or she cannot well bear or profit from without fatigue.

Similarly exercitants should be given, each one, as much as they are willing to dispose themselves to receive, for their greater help and progress.

Consequently, a person who wants help to get some instruction and reach a certain level of peace of soul can be given the Particular Examen ([24–31]), and then the General Examen ([32–43]), and farther, the Method of Praying for a half hour in the morning on the Commandments ([238–243]), the Capital Sins ([244–245]), and other such procedures ([238; 246–260]). Such a person can also be encouraged to weekly confession of sins and, if possible, to reception of the Eucharist every two weeks or, if better disposed, weekly. This procedure is more appropriate for persons who are rather simple or illiterate. They should be given an explanation of each of the commandments, the seven capital sins, the precepts of the Church, the five senses, and the works of mercy.

Likewise, if the one giving the Exercises sees that the recipient is a person poorly qualified or of little natural capacity from whom much fruit is not to be expected, it is preferable to give to such a one some of these light Exercises until he or she has confessed, and then to give ways of examining one's conscience and a program for confession more frequent than before, that the person may preserve what has been acquired. But this should be done without going on to matters pertaining to the Election or to other Exercises beyond the First Week. This is especially the case when there are others with whom greater results can be achieved and time is insufficient to do everything.

[19]   *The Nineteenth. A* person who is involved in public affairs or pressing occupations but educated or intelligent may take an hour and a half each day to perform the Exercises. To such a one the director can explain the end for which human beings are created. Then he or she can explain for half an hour the particular examen, then the general examen, and the method of confessing and receiving the Eucharist. For three days this exercitant should make a mediation for an hour each morning on the first, second, and third sins ([45–53]); then for another three days at the same hour the mediation on the court-record of one's own sins ([55–56]); then for the further three days at the same hour the meditation on the punishment corresponding to sins ([65–72]). During these three meditations the ten Additional Directives ([73–90]) should be given the exercitant. For the mysteries of Christ our Lord this exercitant should follow the same procedure as is explained below and at length throughout the Exercises themselves.

[20]   *The Twentieth. A* person who is more disengaged, and who desires to make all the progress possible, should be given all the Spiritual Exercises in the same sequence in which they proceed below. Ordinarily, in making them an exercitant will achieve more progress the more he or she withdraws from all friends and acquaintances, and from all earthly concerns; for example, by moving out of one's place of residence and taking a different house or room where one can live in the greatest possible solitude, and thus be free to attend Mass and Vespers daily without fear of hindrance from acquaintances. Three principal advantages flow from this seclusion, among many others.

　　First, by withdrawing from friends and acquaintances and likewise from various activities that are not well ordered, in order to serve and praise God our Lord, we gain much merit in the eyes of his Divine Majesty.

Second, by being secluded in this way and not having our mind divided among many matters, but by concentrating instead all our attention on one alone, namely, the service of our Creator and our own spiritual progress, we enjoy a freer use of our natural faculties for seeking diligently what we so ardently desire.

Third, the more we keep ourselves alone and secluded, the more fit do we make ourselves to approach and attain to our Creator and Lord; and the nearer we come to him in this way, the more do we dispose ourselves to received graces and gifts from his divine and supreme goodness.

[21]   **SPIRITUAL EXERCISES**

**TO OVERCOME ONESELF,
AND TO ORDER ONE'S LIFE,
WITHOUT REACHING A DECISION
THROUGH SOME DISORDERED AFFECTION.**

[22]   **PRESUPPOSITION**

That both the giver and the receiver of the Spiritual Exercises may be of greater help and benefit to each other, it should be presupposed that every good Christian ought to be more eager to put a good interpretation on a neighbor's statement than to condemn it. Further, if one cannot interpret it favorably, one should ask how the other means it. If that meaning is wrong, one should correct the person with love; and if this is not enough, one should search out every appropriate means through which, by understanding the statement in a good way, it may be saved.

THE FIRST WEEK

[23]   **PRINCIPLE AND FOUNDATION**

Human beings are created to praise, reverence, and serve God our Lord, and by means of this to save their souls.

The other things on the face of the earth are created for the human beings, to help them in working toward the end for which they are created.

From this it follows that I should use these things to the extent that they help me toward my end, and rid myself of them to the extent that they hinder me.

To do this, I must make myself indifferent to all created things, in regard to everything which is left to my freedom of will and is not forbidden. Consequently, on my own part I ought not to seek health rather than sickness, wealth rather than poverty, honor rather than dishonor, a long life rather than a short one, and so on in all other matters.

I ought to desire and elect only the thing which is more conducive to the end for which I am created.

[24]   **DAILY PARTICULAR EXAMINATION
OF CONSCIENCE.
It comprises three times in the day and two
examinations of conscience.**

The First Time is in the morning. Upon arising the person should resolve to guard carefully against the particular sin or fault he or she wants to correct or amend.

[25]   *The Second Time* is after the noon meal. One should ask God our Lord for what one desires, namely, grace to recall how often one has fallen in to the particular sin or fault, in order to correct it in the future. Then one should make the first examination, exacting an account of oneself with regard to the particular matter one has decided to take for correction and improvement. One should run through the time, hour

by hour or period by period, from the moment of rising until the present examination. On the upper line of the G== one should enter a dot for each time one fell into the particular sin or fault. Then one should renew one's resolution to do better during the time until the second examination which will be made later.

[26] *The Third Time* is after supper. The person should make the second examination, likewise hour by hour starting from the previous examination down to the present one. For each time he or she fell into the particular sin or fault, a dot should be entered on the lower line of the g==.

[27] **FOUR ADDITIONAL DIRECTIVES
to help toward quicker riddance
of the particular sin or fault.**

The First Directive. Each time one falls into the particular sin or fault, one should touch one's hand to one's breast in sorrow for having fallen. This can be done even in public without its being noticed by others.

[28] *The Second.* Since the upper line of the G== represents the first examination and the lower line the second, the person should look at night to see if there was any improvement from the first line to the second, that is, from the first examination to the second.

[29] *The Third.* The person should compare the second day with the first, that is, the two examinations of each day with those of the previous day, to see whether any improvement has been made from one day to the next.

[30] *The Fourth.* The person should compare this week with the previous one, to see if any improvement has been made during the present week in comparison with the one before.

[31]   It should be noted that the first large G== on the top line
       indicates Sunday, the second and smaller g== Monday, the
       third Tuesday, and so on.

       G==========.
       g==========.
       g==========.
       g==========.
       g==========.
       g==========.
       g==========.

[32] GENERAL EXAMINATION OF CONSCIENCE
   to purify oneself, and to make a better confession.

I assume that there are three kinds of thoughts in myself. That
is, one kind is my own, which arises strictly from my own freedom and desire; and the other two come from outside myself,
the one from the good spirit and the other from the evil.

[33]   **Thoughts**

       There are two ways in which I can merit from an evil
thought that comes from outside myself.
       The first occurs when a thought of committing a
mortal sin comes to me, and I resist it immediately, and it
remains banished.

[34]   The second way to merit occurs when this same bad
       thought comes to me, and I resist it, but it keeps coming
       back and I resist it continually, until it is overcome and goes
       away. This second way gains more merit than the first.

[35]   I sin venially when this same thought of committing a mor-
       tal sin comes to me and I give some heed to it—dwelling on
       it somewhat or experiencing some pleasure in the senses; or
       when there is some slackness in repulsing the thought.

[36]   There are two ways of sinning mortally. The first occurs when I consent to the bad thought, intending at that time to carry out what I have assented to, or to do so if it becomes possible.

[37]   The second way of sinning mortally occurs when one actually carries out the sin. This is graver, for three reasons: the longer time involved, the greater intensity, and the worse harm to the two persons.

[38]   **Words**

It is not permissible to swear, either by God or by creature, unless it is done with truth, necessity, and reverence. With necessity, that is, to affirm with an oath, not just any truth at all, but only one of some importance for the good of the soul, or the body, or temporal interests. With reverence, that is, when in pronouncing the name of our Creator and Lord one acts with consideration and manifests that honor and reverence which are due to him.

[39]   In an unnecessary oath, it is a more serious sin to swear by the Creator than by a creature. However, we should note, it is harder to swear by a creature with the proper truth, necessity, and reverence than to swear by the Creator, for the following reasons.

The First. When we desire to swear by a creature, our very desire to name a creature makes us less careful and cautious about speaking the truth or affirming it with necessity than is the case when our urge is to name the Lord and creator of all things.

The Second. When we swear by a creature, it is not as easy to maintain reverence and respect for the Creator as it is when we swear by the name of the Creator and Lord himself. For our very desire to name God our Lord carries with it greater respect and reverence than desire to name a creature. Consequently, to swear by a creature is more permissible for persons spiritually far advanced than for those less advanced. The perfect, through constant contemplation and enlightenment of their understanding, more readily consider, meditate, and contemplate God our Lord as being present in every creature by his essence, presence, and power. Thus when they swear by a creature they are more able and better disposed than the imperfect to render respect and reverence to their Creator and Lord.

The Third. To swear continually by a creature brings a risk of idolatry that is greater in the imperfect than in the perfect.

[40] It is not permissible to speak idle words. I take this to mean words that are of no benefit to myself or anyone else, and are not ordered toward such benefit. Consequently, words that benefit or are intended to benefit my own or another's soul, body, or temporal goods are never idle. Nor are they idle merely because they are about matters outside one's state of life; for example, if a religious talks about wars or commerce. However, in all that has been mentioned, there is merit if the words are ordered to a good end, and sin if they are directed to a bad end, or by one's talking uselessly.

[41] We may not say anything to harm the reputation of others or to disparage them. If I reveal another person's mortal sin that is not publicly known, I sin mortally; if a venial sin, venially; if a defect, I expose my own defect.

When one has a right intention, there are two cases where it is permissible to speak about someone else's sin or fault.

The first. When the sin is public, for example, in the case of a known prostitute, a judicial sentence, or a public error infecting the minds of those with whom we live.

The second. When a hidden sin is revealed to another person so that he or she can help the sinner arise from this state. But in that case there must be conjectures or probable reasons to think that this person will be able to help the sinner.

[42] **Deeds**

Here the subject matter takes in the ten commandments, the precepts of the Church, and the official recommendations of our superiors. Any action performed against these three headings is a sin, more serious or less in accordance with its nature. By official recommendations of our superiors I mean, for example, the bulls about crusades and other indulgences, such as those for peaceful reconciliations on condition of confession and reception of the Eucharist. For it is no small sin to act or cause others to act against these pious exhortations and recommendations of our superiors.

[43] **A METHOD FOR MAKING THE GENERAL EXAMINATION OF CONSCIENCE. It contains five points.**

The First Point is to give thanks to God our Lord for the benefits I have received from him.

The Second is to ask grace to know my sins and rid myself of them.

The Third is to ask an account of my soul from the hour of rising to the present examen, hour by hour or period by period; first as to thoughts, then words, then deeds, in the same order as was given for the particular examination [in 25].

The Fourth is to ask pardon of God our Lord for my faults.

The Fifth is to resolve, with his grace, to amend them. Close with an Our Father.

[44] **GENERAL CONFESSION, WITH HOLY COMMUNION**

For a person who voluntarily desires to make a general confession, to make it here in the time of retreat will bring three benefits, among others.

The First. It is granted that a person who confesses annually is not obliged to make a general confession. Nevertheless, to make it brings greater profit and merit, because of the greater sorrow experienced at present for all the sins and evil deeds of one's entire life.

The Second. During these Spiritual Exercises one reaches a deeper interior understanding of the reality and malice of one's sins than when one is not so concentrated on interior concerns. In this way, by coming to know and grieve for the sins more deeply during this time, one will profit and merit more than was the case on earlier occasions.

*The Third. A*s a result of having made a better confession and come to a better disposition, one is worthier and better prepared to receive the Holy Sacrament. Furthermore, the reception of it helps, not only to avoid falling into sin, but also to preserve the increase of grace.

The general confession is best made immediately after the Exercises of the First Week.

[45]
THE FIRST EXERCISE
IS A MEDITATION
BY USING THE THREE POWERS
OF THE SOUL ABOUT THE FIRST,
SECOND, AND THIRD SINS.
It contains, after a preparatory prayer
and two preludes,
three main points and a colloquy.

[46] *The Preparatory Prayer* is to ask God our Lord for the grace that all my intentions, actions, and operations may be ordered purely to the service and praise of his Divine Majesty.

[47] *The First Prelude* is a composition made by imagining the place. Here we should take notice of the following. When a contemplation or meditation is about something that can

be gazed on, for example, a contemplation of Christ our Lord, who is visible, the composition consists of seeing in imagination the physical place where that which I want to contemplate is taking place. By physical place I mean, for instance, a temple or a mountain where Jesus Christ or Our Lady happens to be, in accordance with the topic I desire to contemplate.

When a contemplation or meditation is about something abstract and invisible, as in the present case about the sins, the composition will be to see in imagination and to consider my soul as imprisoned in this corruptible body, and my whole compound self as an exile in this valley [of tears] among brute animals. I mean, my whole self as composed of soul and body.

[48]   *The Second Prelude* is to ask God our Lord for what I want and desire. What I ask for should be in accordance with the subject matter. For example, in a contemplation on the Resurrection, I will ask for joy with Christ in joy; in a contemplation on the Passion, I will ask for pain, tears, and suffering with Christ suffering.

In the present meditation it will be to ask for shame and confusion about myself, when I see how many people have been damned for committing a single mortal sin, and how many times I have deserved eternal damnation for my many sins.

[49]   *Note.* All the contemplations or meditations ought to be preceded by this same preparatory prayer, which is never changed, and also by the two preludes, which are sometimes changed in accordance with the subject matter.

[50]   *The First Point* will be to use my memory, by going over the first sin, that of the angels; next, to use my understanding, by reasoning about it; and then my will. My aim in remembering and reasoning about all these matters is to bring myself to greater shame and confusion, by comparing the one sin of the angels with all my own many sins. For one sin they

went to hell; then how often have I deserved hell for my many sins!

In other words, I will call to memory the sin of the angels: How they were created in grace and then, not wanting to better themselves by using their freedom to reverence and obey their Creator and Lord, they fell into pride, were changed from grace to malice, and were hurled from heaven into hell. Next I will use my intellect to ruminate about this in greater detail, and then move myself to deeper affections by means of my will.

[51] *The Second Point* will be meditated in the same way. That is, I will apply the three faculties to the sin of Adam and Eve. I will recall to memory how they did long penance for their sin, and the enormous corruption it brought to the human race, with so many people going to hell.

Again in other words, I will call to memory the second sin, that of our first parents: How Adam was created in the plain of Damascus and placed in the earthly paradise; and how Eve was created from his rib; how they were forbidden to eat of the tree of knowledge, but did eat, and thus sinned; and then, clothed in garments of skin and expelled from paradise, they lived out their whole lives in great hardship and penance, deprived of the original justice which they had lost. Next I will use my intellect to reason about this in greater detail, and then use the will, as is described just above.

[52] *The Third Point* will likewise be to use the same method on the third sin, the particular sin of anyone who has gone to hell because of one mortal sin; and further, of innumerable other persons who went there for fewer sins than I have committed.

That is, about this third particular sin too I will follow the same procedure as above. I will call to memory the gravity and malice of the sin against my Creator and Lord; then I will use my intellect to reason about it—how by sinning and acting against the Infinite Goodness the person has been justly condemned forever. Then I will finish by using the will, as was described above.

[53] *Colloquy.* Imagine Christ our Lord suspended on the cross before you, and converse with him in a colloquy: How is it that he, although he is the Creator, has come to make himself a human being? How is it that he has passed from eternal life to death here in time, and to die in this way for my sins?

In a similar way, reflect on yourself and ask: What have I done for Christ? What am I doing for Christ? What ought I to do for Christ?

In this way, too, gazing on him in so pitiful a state as he hangs on the cross, speak out whatever comes to your mind.

[54] A colloquy is made, properly speaking, in the way one friend speaks to another, or a servant to one in authority— now begging a favor, now accusing oneself of some misdeed, now telling one's concerns and asking counsel about them. Close with an Our Father.

★   ★   ★

[136]
THE FOURTH DAY
A MEDITATION ON TWO STANDARDS, THE ONE OF CHRIST, OUR SUPREME COMMANDER AND LORD, THE OTHER OF LUCIFER, THE MORTAL ENEMY OF OUR HUMAN NATURE.

The Preparatory Prayer will be as usual.

[137] *The First Prelude.* This is the history. Here it will be to consider how Christ calls and desires all persons to come under his standard, and how Lucifer in opposition calls them under his.

[138] *The Second Prelude. A* composition, by imagining the place. Here it will be to imagine a great plain in the region of Jerusalem, where the supreme commander of the good

people is Christ our Lord; then another plain in the region of Babylon, where the leader of the enemy is Lucifer.

[139] *The Third Prelude.* It is to ask for what I desire. Here it will be to ask for insight into the deceits of the evil leader, and for help to guard myself against them; and further, for insight into the genuine life which the supreme and truthful commander sets forth, and grace to imitate him.

PART I. THE STANDARD OF SATAN.

[140] *The First Point.* Imagine the leader of all the enemy in that great plain of Babylon. He is seated on a throne of fire and smoke, in aspect horrible and terrifying.

[141] *The Second Point.* Consider how he summons uncountable devils, disperses some to one city and others to another, and thus reaches into the whole world, without missing any provinces, places, states, or individual persons.

[142] *The Third Point.* Consider the address he makes to them: How he admonishes them to set up snares and chains; how first they should tempt people to covet riches (as he usually does, at least in most cases), so that they may more easily come to vain honor from the world, and finally to surging pride. In this way, the first step is riches, the second is honor, and the third is pride; and from these three steps the enemy entices them to any other vices.

PART II. THE STANDARD OF CHRIST.

[143] Similarly, in contrast, gaze in imagination on the supreme and true leader, who is Christ our Lord.

[144] *The First Point.* Consider how Christ our Lord takes his place in that great plain near Jerusalem, in an area which is lowly, beautiful, and attractive.

[145] *The Second Point.* Consider how the Lord of all the world chooses so many persons, apostles, disciples, and the like.

He sends them throughout the whole world, to spread his doctrine among people of every state and condition.

[146]   *The Third Point.* Consider the address which Christ our Lord makes to all his servants and friends whom he is sending on this expedition. He recommends that they endeavor to aid all persons, by attracting them, first, to the highest degree of spiritual poverty and also, if his Divine Majesty would be served and pleased to choose them for it, to no less a degree of actual poverty; second, by attracting them to a desire of reproaches and contempt, since from these results humility.

In this way there will be three steps: the first, poverty in opposition to riches; the second, reproaches or contempt in opposition to honor from the world; and the third, humility in opposition to pride. Then from these three steps they should induce people to all the other virtues.

[147]   *The First Colloquy* should be with Our Lady. I beg her to obtain for me grace to be received under the standard of her Son and Lord; that is, to be received, first, in the highest degree of spiritual poverty and also, if his Divine Majesty would be served and if he should wish to choose me for it, to no less a degree of actual poverty; and second, in bearing reproaches and injuries, that through them I may imitate him more, if only I can do this without sin on anyone's part and without displeasure to his Divine Majesty. Then I will say a Hail Mary.

The Second Colloquy. It will be to ask the same grace from the Son, that he may obtain it for me from the Father. Then I will say the Soul of Christ.

The Third Colloquy will be to ask the same grace from the Father, that he may grant it to me. Then I will say an Our Father.

[148]   *Note.* This exercise will be made at midnight and again after arising. There will also be two repetitions of it, one near the hour of Mass and one near that of Vespers. Each of these

exercises will close with the three colloquies: one with our
Lady, one with the Son, and one with the Father. Then,
before the evening meal, the exercise on the Three Classes
of Persons will be made, as follows.

*   *   *

[RULES FOR THE DISCERNMENT
OF SPIRITS.]

[313]   **RULES TO AID US TOWARD PERCEIVING
AND THEN UNDERSTANDING, AT LEAST
TO SOME EXTENT, THE VARIOUS
MOTIONS WHICH ARE CAUSED IN THE
SOUL: THE GOOD MOTIONS THAT THEY
MAY BE RECEIVED, AND THE BAD THAT
THEY MAY BE REJECTED.**
These rules are more suitable to the First Week.

[314]   *The First Rule.* In the case of persons who are going from
one mortal sin to another, the enemy ordinarily proposes
to them apparent pleasures. He makes them imagine
delights and pleasures of the senses, in order to hold them
fast and plunge them deeper in their sins and vices.

But with persons of this type the good spirit uses a
contrary procedure. Through their habitual sound judgment on problems of morality he stings their consciences
with remorse.

[315]   *The Second.* In the case of persons who are earnestly purging
away their sins, and who are progressing from good to better
in the service of God our Lord, the procedure used is the
opposite of that described in the First Rule. For in this case it
is characteristic of the evil spirit to cause gnawing anxiety, to
sadden, and to set up obstacles. In this way he unsettles them
by false reasons aimed at preventing their progress.

But with persons of this type it is characteristic of the
good spirit to stir up courage and strength, consolations,

tears, inspirations, and tranquility. He makes things easier and eliminates all obstacles so that the persons may move forward in doing good.

[316]   *The Third,* about spiritual consolation. By [this kind of] consolation I mean that which occurs when some interior motion is caused within the soul through which it comes to be inflamed with love of its Creator and Lord. As a result it can love no created thing on the face of the earth in itself, but only in the Creator of them all.

Similarly, this consolation is experienced when the soul sheds tears which move it to love for its Lord— whether they are tears of grief for its own sins, or about the Passion of Christ our Lord, or about other matters directly ordered to his service and praise.

Finally, under the word consolation I include every increase in hope, faith, and charity, and every interior joy which calls and attracts one toward heavenly things and to the salvation of one's soul, by bringing it tranquility and peace in its Creator and Lord.

[317]   *The Fourth,* about spiritual desolation. By [this kind of] desolation I mean everything which is the contrary of what was described in the Third Rule; for example, darkness of soul, turmoil within it, an impulsive motion toward low and earthly things, or disquiet from various agitations and temptations. These move one toward lack of faith and leave one without hope and without love. One is completely listless, tepid, and unhappy, and feels separated from our Creator and Lord.

For just as consolation is contrary to desolation, so too the thoughts which arise from consolation are likewise contrary to those which spring from desolation.

[318]   *The Fifth.* During a time of desolation one should never make a change. Instead, one should remain firm and constant in the proposals and in a decision in which one

was on the day before the desolation, or in a decision in which one was during a previous time of consolation.

For just as the good spirit is chiefly the one who guides and counsels us in time of consolation, so it is the evil spirit who does this in time of desolation. By following his counsels we can never find the way to a right decision.

[319] *The Sixth.* It is taken for granted that in time of desolation we ought not to change our former plans. But it is very helpful to make vigorous changes in ourselves as counter-attack against the desolation, for example, by insisting more on prayer, meditation, earnest self-examination, and some suitable way of doing penance.

[320] *The Seventh.* When we are in desolation we should think that the Lord has left us in order to test us, by leaving us to our own natural powers so that we may prove ourselves by resisting the various agitations and temptations of the enemy. For we can do this with God's help, which always remains available, even if we do not clearly perceive it. Indeed, even though the Lord has withdrawn from us his abundant fervor, augmented love, and intensive grace, he still supplies sufficient grace for our eternal salvation.

[321] *The Eighth.* One who is in desolation should strive to pre-serve himself or herself in patience. This is the counterat-tack against the vexations which are being experienced. One should remember that after a while the consolation will return again, through the diligent efforts against the desolation which were indicated in the Sixth Rule.

[322] *The Ninth.* There are three main reasons for the desolation we experience.

The first is that we ourselves are tepid, lazy, or negli-gent in our spiritual exercises. Thus the spiritual consola-tion leaves us because of our own faults.

The second reason is that the desolation serves to test how much we are worth, that is, how far we will go in the

service and praise of God, even without much compensa-
tion by way of consolations and increased graces.

    The third reason is to give us a true recognition and
understanding, in order to make us perceive interiorly that
we cannot by ourselves bring on or retain increased devotion, intense love, tears, or any other spiritual consolation;
and further, that all these are a gift and grace from God our
Lord; and still further, that they are granted to keep us from
building our nest in a house which belongs to Another, by
puffing up our minds with pride or vainglory through
which we attribute the devotion or other features of spiritual consolation to ourselves.

[323]   *The Tenth.* One who is in consolation should consider how
he or she will act in future desolation, and store up new
strength for that time.

[324]   *The Eleventh.* One who is in consolation ought to humble
and abase himself or herself as much as possible, and reflect
how little he is worth in time of desolation when that grace
or consolation is absent.

    In contrast, one who is in desolation should reflect
that with the sufficient grace already available he or she can
do much to resist all hostile forces, by drawing strength
from our Creator and Lord.

[325]   *The Twelfth.* The enemy conducts himself like a woman. He
is weak against physical strength but strong when confronted by weakness.

    When she is quarreling with a man and he shows
himself bold and unyielding, she characteristically loses her
spirit and goes away. But if the man begins to lose his spirit
and backs away, the woman's anger, vindictiveness, and
ferocity swell almost without limit.

    In the same way, the enemy characteristically weak-
ens, loses courage, and flees with his temptations when
the person engaged in spiritual endeavors stands bold
and unyielding against the enemy's temptations and goes

---

diametrically against them. But if, in contrast, that person begins to fear and lose courage in the face of the temptations, there is no beast on the face of the earth as fierce as the enemy of human nature when he is pursuing his damnable intention with his surging malice.

[326]   *The Thirteenth.* Similarly the enemy acts like a false lover, insofar as he tries to remain secret and undetected. For such a scoundrel, speaking with evil intent and trying to seduce the daughter of a good father or the wife of a good husband, wants his words and solicitations to remain secret. But he is deeply displeased when the daughter reveals his deceitful words and evil design to her father, or the wife to her husband. For he easily infers that he cannot succeed in the design he began.

In a similar manner, when the enemy of human nature turns his wiles and persuasions upon an upright person, he intends and desires them to be received and kept in secrecy. But when the person reveals them to his or her good confessor or some other spiritual person who understands the enemy's deceits and malice, he is grievously disappointed. For he quickly sees that he cannot succeed in the malicious project he began, because his manifest deceptions have been detected.

[327]   *The Fourteenth.* To use still another comparison, the enemy acts like a military commander who is attempting to conquer and plunder his objective. The captain and leader of an army on campaign sets up his camp, studies the strength and structure of a fortress, and then attacks at its weakest point.

In the same way, the enemy of human nature prowls around and from every side probes all our theological, cardinal, and moral virtues. Then at the point where he finds us weakest and most in need in regard to our eternal salvation, there he attacks and tries to take us.

Chapter 2

FINDING MEANING BY LOOKING WITHIN:

AUGUSTINE OF HIPPO

Few people in today's world, especially those living in the West, would find it strange to think that the path to ultimate meaning lies within. Twentieth-century psychology has made us very accustomed to that idea. Sigmund Freud, the father of modern psychoanalysis, told us that understanding ourselves required looking within to see the ways in which our libidinal energies, emanating from a part of the personality known as the Id, influenced our conscious behavior and our social choices. Carl Jung taught that each of us possessed a collective unconscious that influenced many of our behaviors. The concept of the unconscious is itself a statement that within us lie unchartered lands. Freud and Jung, and the whole school they founded, agree that mental well-being, happiness, self-actualization—and a host of other terms meaning much the same thing—can only be found by turning within.

The turn within to find meaning has always been a big part of American culture. In the nineteenth century, when Americans were defining an uniquely American approach to the arts and sciences, thinkers like Ralph Waldo Emerson and Henry David Thoreau made much of self-reliance. Emerson went so far as to break with traditional Christianity and counsel that each person "declare himself a new born bard of the Holy Spirit." By looking within, one could find all the meaning one required, even when it came to questions about transcendence. Thoreau, following a similar tack, went out to Walden Pond to follow a discipline of self-examination, believing that gaining greater self-mastery was the key to meaning. In his book, *The Naked Heart,* historian Peter Gay looks at the thoughts and feelings of the nineteenth-century middle class. He charts the Victorian obsession with the self and argues that the psychoanalytical movement of the early twentieth century represented the culmination of a "century-long effort to map inner space."[2]

The late twentieth century saw no abatement of this emphasis on inner feelings. The New Age movement emphasized this approach to finding meaning. A recent catalog from a bookseller listed over 15,000 books under the New Age category. Fundamental to New Age thinking is a belief that the self contains untapped potentials whether for healing, thinking, sexual performance, job success, or just plain feeling good. Part of the new paradigm shift talked about by New Agers involves the change away from outer-directed to inner-directed structures, where people have greater freedom to choose what they feel is more in keeping with their inner compasses.

Even today's interest in health may be seen as part of this larger theme of looking within to find meaning. Our virtual preoccupation with the shape, size, and functions of our bodies appears as a particularly myopic view of things unless one sees it as something more than vanity. It shares in this larger belief that by learning more about our inner workings we can lead better lives. The diet, exercise, and fitness mania partake of this aura.

Although Peter Gay is right in showing that the nineteenth century saw a new preoccupation with the self, the idea of looking within to find meaning has a very long history in Western culture. It dates back at least as far as Socrates, whose famous maxim, "the unexamined life is not worth living," implied a heuristic method that rested on the conviction that the soul was the storehouse of all knowledge and that learning consisted in drawing out the understanding that lay within. Certainly one of the most influential contributors to this approach was Augustine. As the writer of what is undoubtedly the most popular autobiography ever written, the *Confessions,* his influence and his value reach to our own day.

---

2. Peter Gay, *The Naked Heart* (New York: W. W. Norton & Co., 1995), p. 4.

AUGUSTINE'S LIFE AND TIMES

Augustine was born in 354 in the Numidian town of Thagaste, in what is now northeast Algeria. Son of a middle-class patrician farmer, he grew up in comfort during the closing days of the Roman Empire. Rome, the colossus of the Mediterranean world, was in a state of decline during the late fourth century. The erosion of its political power by conflicts within the central government led to the division of the Empire into East and West in 395. In addition, well-organized belligerent tribes threatened the frontiers.

The ferment of political and economic change was accompanied by cultural transformation. Hellenism, the Roman adaptation of the culture of the ancient Greeks, was still the dominant force in the intellectual life of the time. It was supported by a system of philosophy that kept alive the thought of Plato, Aristotle, and the lesser teachers like Cicero, Epicurus, and Marcus Aurelius. Paganism, with its veneration of Roman gods and its cult of emperor worship, served the Hellenic culture well, providing a symbolic structure for its most cherished values.

In that context Christianity emerged first as a variant of Judaism but later under St. Paul as a new faith for the Gentile pagans. Initially, the new religion made its greatest mark among the poor and other marginal elements of Roman society who found hope in Paul's teaching: "...there is neither Jew nor Greek, bond nor free, male nor female but you are all one in Christ Jesus." With time the new faith spread to the higher classes. That movement culminated in 312 with the legalization of the Christian sect within the Roman Empire. With the Edict of Nicea, Christianity became a legitimate part of mainstream Roman culture. This legal standing, however, was no assurance that it would be taken seriously by the pagan intellectuals, who saw themselves as guardians of the Hellenic tradition.

The movement to legitimate Christian thought in the Hellenic world began only a century before Augustine's birth in the work of Origen (ca. 185–253). It gathered force in the fourth century with the Cappapocian Fathers, Gregory of Nyssa, Gregory of Nazianzen, and St. Basil, and was in full bloom in Augustine's contemporary, St. Ambrose, bishop of Milan. Augustine lived in a world in which Christianity, if it were to survive and expand, had to take Hellenistic philosophy seriously.

For Augustine that interaction of Hellenism and Christianity was a natural concern, for he had been educated in the philosophy of the Greeks, and, although his mother Monica was a Christian, he never had been baptized. He had left his native Thagaste as a young man to study and teach rhetoric in Carthage. There he read the works of Cicero, especially his *Hortensius,* which presented the idea that the life of the mind was superior to that of the senses. That idea set him on the philosophical quest. Augustine believed that the pursuit of wisdom was the most honorable, and ultimately most happy life.

Augustine was a man alive to the pleasures of this life. His writing betrays a great soul that passionately loved life, cherished his friendships, and deeply felt the pain of alienation and disharmony. Unlike Origen, who had solved the problem of dealing with his sexual drives by castrating himself in literal obedience to the saying of Jesus that "there are some who become eunuchs for the kingdom of God's sake," Augustine could never sacrifice his sexuality to zeal. For many years, while he drew nearer and nearer to a full acceptance of the Christian message, he lived with a concubine by whom he had a son, Adeodatus. When he finally did separate from that woman it was done less out of conscience than in preparation for a legitimate marriage to another of his own class. His arrangement with his concubine was not unlike the many trial marriages of today in which unmarried persons cohabit. Those unions are on the margins of legitimacy, thought by some to be upright, while others doubt their moral worth. So it was that Augustine's concubinage in his day was a challenge to the traditional moral views of the status quo.

During his time in Milan Augustine was struggling with his own divided heart. On the one hand, he wished to seek God with his whole self, to follow the way of Christianity he had heard preached with such brilliance by Ambrose. On the other, he was genuinely attracted to the delights of the senses. As much as he was convinced that the higher life of philosophy, as he had learned it from Cicero, was superior to a life in service to bodily pleasures, he found that his good intentions often were not enough. A power pulled him down that he seemed unable to escape and was working against his efforts to live the higher life. As a Hellenistic thinker, Augustine accepted the Greek notion that the soul was superior to the body and must control the body.

One afternoon he was walking in the garden of his villa, pondering his dilemma. He felt an inner compulsion to retire to a private place and pray. Finding a place under a fig tree, he fell on the ground and began to beseech God for an answer to his problem, which by this time was causing him great consternation. At that moment, he heard what he described simply as the voice of a messenger of God that said: *tolle lege,* take and read. Going back to the villa, he went to the New Testament and opened it. His eyes were riveted on the thirteenth chapter of the book of Romans on St. Paul's exhortation: "Put on the Lord Jesus Christ and make no provision for the flesh in regard to its lusts." At that moment the battle that had been raging in Augustine was decided. He sought baptism and devoted himself fully to living the life of the Gospel. Together with a small group of friends and relatives, he returned to his native town of Thagaste and lived in community.

In 395 he moved to the North African town of Hippo, where he was made bishop. He served in that capacity for forty years, all the time mixing his pastoral duties with his writing.

His writing career was fruitful even by modern standards: 113 books, 218 letters, and 800 sermons. His work included polemical books in which he argued for the truth of Christianity against the rival philosophies of Pelagianism and Paganism. He composed great theological works like his masterpiece *On the Trinity,* in which he explored with unparalleled insight the great mystery of Christianity. He wrote commentaries on biblical books and moral treatises, such as *On the Morals of the Catholic Faith*. Toward the end of his life, he composed a history of the world in which he traced the action of God in human events. *The City of God* is a classic of both theology and political science. But his most famous work was a book about his own spiritual journey. The *Confessions* is, next to the Bible, the most widely read piece of Christian literature in history. Through it Augustine's teachings and, as we shall see, his basic approach to the spiritual life were promulgated. In addition to his books, he composed a Rule that outlined the basic structure for communities of Christians to follow. It became the foundation for monasticism in the West and is still followed by groups today.

AUGUSTINE'S MESSAGE

The Two Wills

It is clear from his writing that Augustine was a man who genuinely loved life. His move from a life dominated by the senses to one dominated by the spirit was an arduous one. It was not motivated by a hatred for the world of the senses, as many have wrongly alleged on the basis of his doctrine of Original Sin. His conception of human nature was optimistic, even idyllic. It was not hatred but love that moved Augustine on his journey.

That does not erase the differences between Augustine and those who think that the problem with Western morality is that it opposes soul and body, and that Augustine is primarily responsible for bringing that notion into Christianity. Without a doubt, he believed in and vigorously defended the hierarchical view of creation in which the soul is superior to the body and must reign over it. For Augustine, the battle to control one's body was not just an internal scrimmage with low stakes but a battle of good against evil.

In Book VII of his *Confessions,* Augustine tells how he became sensitive to the problem of evil and pondered over and over the question: What is the origin of evil? He knew evil in a very direct and personal way. He saw it not only in the external forces of corruption that worked in nature or in the behavior of the unjust but in his own life as well. He felt it motivating him, even though his reason compelled him in another direction. What was unusual about him was not that he experienced evil, but that he was obsessed with trying to avoid it. He wanted to know whether it were really possible to live a better life or whether his aspirations were simply the fatuous dreams of youth. This desire led him to a group that followed the ideas of the philosopher Manichee. Under their influence he embraced the idea that God had created the universe out of evil matter. There existed two substances: the evil material world and the good spiritual world. The soul of man was spirit entrapped in the evil material world, from which it could escape ultimately only by separation of the soul from the body.

But as Augustine drew nearer to accepting the Christian message, he came to reject the Manichean explanation as erroneous: "I inquired what wickedness was and I found that it was not a substance, but a swerving of the will from the highest substance, you, O God, toward lower things, casting away what is most inward to it and swelling greedily for outward things" [10.16]. For God, then, nothing that he created was evil. Evil entered the world only when his creatures chose not to seek the highest good and to love instead those things that had been created for a lower order of being. For example, there was nothing evil about the beauty of a woman. But when Augustine loved that beauty more than the Ultimate Beauty, God, he became entrapped in the well-formed things of the world that hindered the ascent of his soul to God, for whom it was made, and only in whom it could find ultimate satisfaction.

The world of the senses, as rich as it could be at one moment, would ultimately disappoint. Philosophy had taught him that whoever has what he wants is happy. But the things of the sense world, which one acquires, are constantly passing away. Entropy works to diminish them. The things of the soul are better, however, because they are not subject to the vicissitudes of this world. To possess spiritual things, it is necessary to desire to do what is good, or in other words, to do God's will. To do God's will and to desire only what is good is the path to true and eternal happiness.

But always to will the good is difficult, and Augustine found himself often struggling with a divided will. On the one hand, he knew that the spiritual life was better, and he knew that to be true to it he had to behave in accord with the highest directives of his conscience. On the other hand, he found a contrary power present: concupiscence. Concupiscence wanted the short-term pleasures of the senses. It cared little for virtue; it was oblivious to the needs of others and to the dictates of reason and justice and rejected moderation and continence.

We who live in the post-Freudian world are aware of the divided will. Only we see it in very different terms than did Augustine. In the Freudian model, the ramifications of which still permeate our popular culture, the will to good, or altruism, is really only part of a greater drive: the will to gratifying our libidinal energies. Everything that the human being does moves toward that end. Good deeds are differentiated from bad only by the judgment of society, whose standards form our consciences. The good thing is only a socially acceptable way of gratifying our libido. There is no basis for morality other than social convention, certainly none in the order of things itself. The happy Freudian life consists of developing socially acceptable ways of gratifying one's Id.

For Augustine, in contrast, the happy life requires that we change the object of our desire, that we move from infatuation with sensible forms to love for the divine source and essence itself. That change must be radical, for the divided will can never attain intimate friendship with God. It is too distracted by the many to recognize the one, too tossed by the ups and downs of life to ever get beyond the sparks to the flame itself.

The Turn Within

One moves from a life dominated by the senses to a full awareness of the spiritual realities by turning within. Just as the external material world is not the source of evil, neither is it the ultimate source of good. This realization, this turning away from the materialism of the Manicheans, caused him to turn within. As he wrote: "Being admonished by all of this to return to myself, I entered into my inmost part, with you as leader. I entered within and saw, with my soul's eye, an unchangeable light." The journey within was ultimately an ascent to God who dwelt in the secret place of the heart.

He had been drawn to God by a natural desire for what is good, true, and beautiful. He ascended from the body to the sense-power and from sense-power to intellectual judgment, by which he acknowledged the eternity of Truth above his changing mind. That "unchangeable light," that flash of a glance by which he arrived at That Which Is, filled him with a desire ever to dwell in its presence. As he put it in one of the most memorable passages in all of Western literature:

> Late have I loved you, O Beauty so ancient yet so new, late have I loved you! And behold, you were within me and I was outside, and there I sought for you, and in my deformity I rushed headlong into the well-formed things that you have made. You were with me, and I was not with you. Those outward beauties held me far from you, yet if they had not been in you, they would not have existed at all. You called and cried out to me and broke open my deafness; you shone forth upon me and you scattered my blindness. You breathed fragrance, and I drew in my breath and I now pant for you. I tasted and I hunger and thirst. You touched me, and I burn for your peace. (*Confessions* 10:27)

Augustine, having expressed the turn within with a poetic brilliance that has inspired seekers for sixteen centuries, became the greatest spokesman in Western Christianity of the school of image mysticism. While some stressed seeing God in the creation, and others emphasized finding him through the revelation of Holy Scripture, Augustine was the great advocate of finding God in the inner person. Although he wrote in a distant age, his method of ascent to God through introspection has become the most salient form of spirituality in the modern world.

Remembering the Image

Augustine believed that within each person lies the *capax Dei,* the "capacity for God." That capacity makes it possible for the human person to be re-formed into the image of the Trinity. That process of enlightenment and conversion involves the awareness and consent of the individual, but also, as we shall see below, the gratuitous action of God who reaches out to us in love. We are re-formed to intimacy with our true selves and to close, loving communion with God and with others. Made in a formless unlikeness to God, humanity can be re-formed into the Image by returning to the One, according to its capacity.

In what is his most original contribution to the Christian mystical tradition, Augustine attempted to fathom the mystery of the human self and the mystery of the Trinity in relation to each other. The Trinity is imaged in the soul. Just as the different parts of the self—the memory, the understanding, and the will—form a unity, so do the Father, Son, and Holy Spirit. Our own being, in its innermost secrets, is itself a reflection of an even greater mystery: the mystery of the Godhead. We participate in God in a profound and essential manner. Not simply by reason of what we believe, or what we say, or what we do, but by the very fact of our being are we united to God, joined to him in our origin and our destiny. Our quest for self-understanding is—whatever else we might think it—ultimately a quest for God. Entering into ourselves we ascend to the heights of the Godhead.

In his work *On the Trinity* Augustine worked out the ramifications of his Image doctrine. As abstract as the ideas that follow may seem, they relate directly to Augustine's main question: How do I live a life of virtue? Since he believes that there is an organic link between human nature and God, he begins his discussion with what he thinks is the natural structure and function of the mind. He then takes that model and shows how it relates to the Trinity. If we understand one, we will understand the other. His whole introspective approach is based on that confidence. He spoke of Trinity in three ways: the mental trinity, which he presents as the model for the natural structure and function of the mind; the trinity of the mind as image of the Father, Son, and Holy Spirit; and the Trinity as that which we actually participate in at the highest stages of spiritual growth.

First he described what he called the mental trinity, his model of the normal thinking process by which the mind perceives an object in the external world and integrates that perception in the act of thinking. He highlighted three aspects of the self in this analysis: the memory, the understanding, and the will. In the normal functioning of our mind, those three elements each work together. The memory provides the source from which the thinker's understanding receives a form when the will joins the two together in the act of cognition. For example, we see a round spherical object sailing through the air and we begin trying to understand what it is that we are seeing. Our memory provides us with the idea of "ball." At that moment by an act of our will we say, yes: what I remember about "ball" and what I am thinking about now as I look at that object are the same thing.

When this happens the mind is in one sense seeing itself in the act of thought. That is to say, it is seeing that it already knew what a ball was, even though it was not thinking about it before. In that process it understands and knows itself better. But this begetting of self-knowledge when it sees itself as understood in thought, does not mean that previously it did not know itself. It was known as realities present in memory are known, though not thought about.

This process by which the mind comes to know itself, and not merely learn about the external objects it perceives, is the second sense in which Augustine talks about a trinity. In this union of three mental faculties of memory, understanding, and will we see an image of the Father, Son, and Holy Spirit as they relate to one another in the Godhead.

The memory is the treasure-house of things acquired through the senses. It is also a latent memory, very much like what we might call the unconscious. We find in that more profound depth of the memory those things that we think of for the first time. It is the source of our creativity, the place from which that new word, that new insight comes, that is, in Augustine's words, "a knowledge of knowledge, vision of vision, and understanding of understanding." In one sense then, the insight that comes through our own understanding has its origins in this latent memory, this unconscious pool.

Our memory corresponds to the Father, the begetter, who is the primordial source of all things. He is the creator from whom all things come and in whom they all subsist.

If the memory is the image of the Father, then the individual, who has turned within searching for his true self, will encounter the visage of the Father in his memory. The knowledge of God is present in the memory, even when the memory does not think of it. That knowledge is an unconscious force that activates the longings of the soul for God. It is what makes the soul restive until it rests in God. The great irony of the human condition is for man "to be without Him without Whom he cannot exist"; that man can be unaware of the organic link with the creator. We can live in alienation from our true selves, blotting out the memory of God. Hence Augustine's famous lament from the *Confessions:* "You were with me, but I was not with myself."

The understanding is the faculty by which we come to understand by actually thinking, that is, when our thinking takes form through the begetting of what was present to the memory but not thought of. It is the process of self-understanding by which the mind comes to understand itself more fully in the moment of cognition.

The understanding corresponds to the Son, the begotten, the self-realization of God, the revelation of the Godhead, the Word of God by which the Father was made known.

The will signifies the force by which the knowledge, present in the memory, and the understanding, produced in the act of thinking about a given thing, are united. The will to unite the two stems from our attraction to a given object, often our affection or love. The will corresponds to the Spirit, the bond of unity between the Father and the Son, the fire of love that unites them, the power that inspires them.

The last sense in which Augustine talks about a trinity is to speak of the way in which the person, at the highest levels of spiritual development is able, not only to see in his mind an image of the Trinity, but actually to participate in the very life of the Godhead. When the mind begins to remember God, to become aware of that knowledge of God, and to love God, the person begins to interact not simply with an archetype, not simply with an analogy, but with True Being Itself. That process Augustine describes as follows:

> And when its [the soul's] cleaving to Him has become absolute, it will be one spirit with Him: Witness the words of the Apostle, "He that is joined to the Lord is one spirit" by drawing near, in order to participate in that being, truth, and bliss….Joined to that Being in perfect happiness, the mind will live with that Being a changeless life, enjoying the changeless vision of all it beholds. (*De Trin.* XIV. 14. 20)

This is in no way something that happens in one moment, such as the moment of conversion. Conversion is only the beginning; it is only the start of the process of healing, like removing a sliver from a wound. It is, in fact, a lifelong process that will only be perfected when we see God, as St. Paul says not "through a glass dimly, but face to face." It is our destiny to fulfill the words of the Gospel of John: "We shall be like him, for we shall see him like he is."

The Role of Grace

That movement of the soul toward God is not only the work of the will desiring to love God and be one with him. It is primarily the action of the Trinity itself reaching out to us, transforming us, remaking us in its own Image. Augustine is, for good reason, known as "the Doctor of Grace." It was precisely the notion that God could do more for us than we could ever do for ourselves that motivated him to become a Christian, rather than to remain a follower of Neo-platonist thought. He could find in Plotinus the idea of the return of the soul to the one; he could find there also the idea of participation in the unchanging world of the one. What he could not find there was the means by which such lofty goals could be reached.

Christ, he came to believe, is the great mediator between God and man. Christ is the Father's gift, his reaching out to humanity by taking on human nature; his participation in human life, the way for us to the full life of communion with True Being. In the tenth book of the *Confessions* he writes of an experience in which he heard, as it were, a voice from on high saying: "I am the food of grown men; grow and you will feed on me. You will not change me into yourself, as with ordinary food; but you will be changed into me" (*Conf.* VII.10). With this confidence, he could pray in another of his memorable utterings: "Give what you require, and require whatever you will."

This synergism between human and divine will, this utter reliance upon God's action, yet complete confidence in the naturalness of the link between God and the soul is a hallmark of Augustine's thought.

BIBLIOGRAPHY

Texts

Augustine of Hippo: Selected Writings. Translated by Mary T. Clark. The Classics of Western Spirituality. New York/Mahwah, N.J.: Paulist Press, 1984.

The Literal Meaning of Genesis. Translated by John H. Taylor. Ancient Christian Writers series. New York/Mahwah, N.J.: Paulist Press, 1982.

Studies

Brown, Peter. *Augustine of Hippo: A Biography.* Berkeley: University of California Press, 1967.

Burnaby, John. *Amor Dei: A Study of Religion of St. Augustine.* London: Hodder and Stoughton, 1938.

Pope, Hugh. *The Teaching of St. Augustine on Prayer and the Contemplative Life.* London: Burns, Oates and Washbourne, 1935.

Confessions[3]

BOOK EIGHT

6

And how you delivered me from the chains of my desire for sex by which I was so closely bound and from the servitude to worldly affairs, I shall declare and confess to your name, O Lord, my Helper and my Redeemer. As I led my usual life, anxiety grew greater and greater, and every day I sighed to you. I visited your church as much as I was allowed by my business, under the burden of which I groaned. Alypius was now with me, at leisure from his law work after the third time as Assessor, awaiting clients to whom he might sell his counsel, as I used to sell the power of speaking if such power can be taught. Nebridius, however, as an act of friendship had agreed to lecture under Verecundus, a great friend of ours, a citizen and elementary-school master of Milan who eagerly wanted Nebridius's assistance and by the right of friendship even demanded from one of our group the faithful aid which he greatly needed. Nebridius was not drawn to this by any desire of profit—for he could have done better for himself by teaching literature, if he pleased—but as a good and gentle friend he was too kindly a man to turn down our request. But he did it very discreetly, desirous of being unknown to persons of worldly reputation, avoiding all disturbance of mind, for he wished to have a free mind and as many hours of leisure as possible to seek or read or hear truths concerning wisdom.

---

3. *Augustine of Hippo: Selected Writings,* trans. Mary T. Clark, the Classics of Western Spirituality (New York/Mahwah, N.J.: Paulist Press, 1984).

Therefore on a certain day—I do not recall why Nebridius was absent—behold there came to our house, to me and Alypius, a certain Ponticianus, our fellow-citizen, an African, holder of an important office at the court of the Emperor. He had something or other he wanted from us, and we sat down to talk about it. Nearby was a game table and he happened to notice the book lying there; he took it, opened it and found it to be the Apostle Paul, certainly contrary to what he expected to find; for he thought it would be one of those books I wore myself out teaching. Smiling then and gazing closely at me, he expressed pleasure as well as surprise that I had this book and only this book at my side. For he was a Christian and a faithful one, and often prostrated himself before you, our God, in church in daily prayers, and many times daily. I indicated to him that I was greatly concerned with those Scriptures. Then he began to tell the story of Anthony the monk of Egypt, whose name was esteemed among your servants although we had not until then heard of him. When he discovered this, he talked about him all the more, eager to make known so great a man to those who knew him not, and very much marveling at our ignorance. But Alypius and I were amazed to hear of your wonderful works, done in the true faith and in the Catholic Church so recently, indeed, practically in our own time and witnessed to by so many. We all marveled—we, that such great things were done, he, that we had never heard of them before.

He went on to speak of the great groups living in monasteries, of their way of life which was full of the sweet fragrance of you and of the fruitful deserts in the wilderness of which we knew nothing. There was actually a monastery at Milan, outside the city's walls. It was full of good brethren and was under Ambrose's direction, and we had never heard of it. He continued to speak and we listened intently. Then he began to say that he and three other comrades—I know not when—at Treves when the emperor was busy with circus chariot races, went walking in the gardens near the city walls; and it so happened that they separated into two groups, one walking with him and the other two going off by themselves. But as these two were wandering up and down, they stumbled by chance upon a certain small house where dwelt some of your servants, "poor in spirit, of which is the Kingdom of Heaven" (Mt 5:5) and they found there a book in which was written the Life of Anthony. One of the two began to read it, to marvel and be inflamed, and while reading to ponder on his own living of such a life and forsaking his military pursuits, serving you. For these two men were both officials in the emperor's civil service. Then suddenly filled with holy love, and a sober shame, angry with himself, he looked at his friend and said "Tell me, I beg you, for what post of honor are we striving with all our labors? What are we seeking? Why are we serving the State? Can our hopes in court rise higher than to become the emperor's friends? And is not such a place insecure and full of danger? And through how many dangers must we go to arrive at a greater danger? And how long will it take to get there? But if I want, I can be the friend of God now, this moment." He said this and perplexed in the labor of a new life to which he was giving birth he looked again at the book. He read on and was inwardly changed where you alone could see, and his mind was emptied of worldly affairs as was soon made evident. For while he read and the waves of his heart rose and fell, he expressed his self-anger, saw the better way, and chose it for himself. And having become yours, he said to his friend: "Now I have torn myself from those hopes of ours, and have decided to serve God; and this—from this moment in this place I shall undertake. If you are unwilling to imitate me, do not dissuade me." The other answered that he would remain his companion in so great a service for so great a prize. And both, now yours, built a spiritual tower at the only adequate cost, that of leaving all things and following you.

Then Ponticianus and the one with him who had walked through other parts of the garden seeking for their friends came upon them and warned that they should return because the day was ending. But they declared to them their resolutions and purpose and told them how that will had arisen in them and was now fixed, and they begged their friends, if they would not join them, not to interfere with their purpose. Ponticianus and his friend, though not changed from their former state, nevertheless wept, for themselves, as he told us, piously wishing them well and recommending themselves to their prayers; and with their hearts still turned toward earthly things, they returned to the court. But the other two, with their hearts fixed on heaven, remained in that cottage. And both of them were to be married; when their fiancées heard what had happened, they also dedicated their virginity to you.

7

This was the story Ponticianus told. But you, O Lord, while he was speaking turned me around to face myself, taking me from behind my back, where I had placed myself when I was reluctant to see myself; and you set me in front of my own face that I might see how deformed, how crooked and sordid, stained and ulcerous I was. I saw and I was horrified and found no way to flee from myself. And if I tried to turn away my gaze from myself, he continued to relate this story. And you set me in front of myself and thrust me before my own eyes so that I might discover my iniquity and hate it. I was aware of it, but I pretended to be unaware. I deliberately looked the other way and dropped it from my mind.

Then indeed the more ardently I loved those young men as I heard of their determination to win health for their souls by giving themselves totally to your healing, the more bitterly I hated myself in comparison with them: Since I had already squandered so many years—about twelve—since my nineteenth year, when, having read Cicero's *Hortensius,* I was first stirred up to study wisdom, and I was still postponing the contempt of earthly happiness and the inquiry into that of which not only the finding but even the search should have been preferred before the already found treasures and kingdoms of this world and before all bodily pleasures readily available. But I, wretched young man that I was, even more wretched in my early youth, had begged chastity from you and had said: "Give me chastity and continence but not yet." For I feared that you

would hear me too soon and too soon deliver me from my disease
of concupiscence which I wrongly desired to have satisfied rather
than extinguished. And I had gone along evil ways, following a
sacrilegious superstition through the wicked ways of Manichaeism
not because I was convinced by it but because I preferred it to the
Christian teachings into which I did not inquire in a religious
spirit but merely opposed in a spirit of malice.

I had thought that the reason I postponed from day to day
forsaking worldly hope to follow you was only because there did
not seem any certain goal to which to direct my course. But now
the day had come when I stood naked in my own sight and when
my own conscience accused me: "Why is my voice not heard?"
Surely you are the man who used to say that for an uncertain truth
you could not cast off the baggage of vanity. Behold there is now
certainty and that burden still weighs upon you. Others have
received wings to liberate their shoulders from the load, others
who have neither worn themselves out searching nor spent more
than ten years considering it. So I was being gnawed at inside and
vehemently confused with horrible shame while Ponticianus went
on with his story. But when he finished both his speech and his
business, he went his way and I retired into myself, nor did I leave
anything unsaid against myself. With what lashes of accusations did
I not scourge my soul so that it might follow me trying to follow
you? My soul hung back. It refused to follow and yet found no
excuse for not following. All its arguments had already been used
and refuted. There remained only trembling silence, for it feared as
very death the cessation of that habit of which it was wasting away
unto death.

8

Then in the midst of the great tempest of my inner dwelling,
a tempest which I had so vigorously excited against my own soul
in the chamber of my heart, wild both in mind and countenance, I
rushed upon Alypius, exclaiming: "What is wrong with us? What is

this which you have heard? The unlearned rise up and take heaven by violence, and we with all our learning, behold, how we wallow in flesh and blood! Because they have preceded, does it shame us to follow or is it not a shame not to follow them?" Some such words I said and in my rage I broke away from him while, astonished, he said nothing, gazing after me. For I did not sound like myself.

My forehead, my cheeks, my eyes, my flesh, the tone of my voice, expressed my mind more than the words I uttered. There was a garden attached to our house which we used as we did the whole house, for the master of the house did not live there. There the tempest in my breast drove me, there where no one would impede the fierce suit which I had brought against myself until it could be settled—in what way you knew but I did not. But there I was, going mad on my way to sanity, dying on my way to life; aware how evil I was, unaware of how much better I was to be in a little while. Therefore, I withdrew into the garden and Alypius followed close after me. For I was no less in privacy when he was near. And how could he forsake me in such a state? We sat down as far from the house as we could. My mind was frantic, I was boiling with indignation at myself for not going over to your law and your covenant, O my God, where all my bones cried out that I should be, extolling it to the skies. And the way there is not by ship or chariot or on foot. The distance is not as great as I had come from the house to that place where we were now sitting. For to go there and to arrive fully required nothing other than the will to go, but to will strongly and totally, not to turn and twist a half-wounded will this way and that with one part rising up and struggling with the other part that would keep to the earth.

Finally in the torment of my irresolution I made many movements with my body which sometimes men want to make and cannot, if either they have not the limbs to make them or if those limbs be bound with cords, weakened by infirmity, or in some way hindered. If I pulled at my hair, beat my forehead, locked my fingers together, if I clasped my knee within my hand, all this I did because I willed to do it. But I might have willed it and not have done it, if the movement of my limbs had not followed the dictates of my will. Therefore, I did many things when the will was not identical with the power; and I did not do that which would have far more pleased me, which soon after, when I should have the will, I should have the power to do because when I willed, I should will it wholly. For there the power was one with the will, and the very willing was the doing. Yet it was not done and the body more easily obeyed the slightest wish of the mind that the limbs should immediately move than my mind obeyed itself so as to carry out its own great will which could be accomplished simply by willing.

9

How explain this absurdity? What is the cause of it? Let your mercy enlighten me so that I might ask whether the answer lies in the mysterious punishment that has come upon men and in some deeply hidden damage in the sons of Adam. Why this absurdity? And how explain it? The mind commands the body, and is immediately obeyed; the mind commands itself and is resisted. The mind commands the hand to move and the readiness is so great that the commanding is scarcely distinguishable from the doing. Yet the mind is mind whereas the hand is body. The mind commands the mind to will, the mind is itself, but it does not obey. Why this absurdity? And what is its cause? I say that the mind commands itself to will; it would not give the command unless it willed; yet it does not do what it commands. The reason is that it does not wholly will: Therefore it does not wholly command. It commands insofar as it wills, and it disobeys the command insofar as it does not will. The will is commanding itself to be a will, commanding itself, not another. But it does not wholly give the command; therefore that is not done which it commanded. For if the will were wholly itself, a unity, it would not command itself to will because it would already will. It is therefore no absurdity, partly to will, partly not to will, but it is only a sickness of soul to be so weighed down by habit that even when supported by truth it cannot totally rise up. And so there are two wills in us because neither of them is whole, and one has what the other lacks.

10

Let them vanish from your sight, O God, as they do vanish, these vain babblers and seducers of the mind who because they have noticed that there are two wills in the act of deliberating conclude that there are in us two minds of two different natures—one good, the other evil. They themselves are truly evil when they believe these evil opinions, and these same men could be good if they were to realize the truth and consent to the truth so that your apostle may say to them: "Once upon a time you were darkness, but now you are light in the Lord" (Eph 5:8). But these people want to be light not in the Lord but in themselves when they think that the nature of the soul is what God is. Thus they have become deeper darkness since they withdrew further from you in horrid arrogance, from you, the "true Light, enlightening every man coming into this world" (Jn 1:9). Take care what you say and blush for shame: "Draw near to Him and be enlightened and your faces shall not blush for shame" (Ps 34:5). As for me, when I deliberated about serving the Lord my God as I long meant to do, it was I who willed it, I who was unwilling. It was always the same I. I neither willed wholly nor was wholly unwilling. Therefore I struggled with myself and was torn apart by myself. This tearing apart took place against my will, yet this did not prove that I had a second mind of a different nature; but it was merely the punishment suffered by my own mind. Thus I did not cause it but the "sin dwells in me," and since I am a son of Adam, I was suffering from his freely committed sin.

For if there are as many contrary natures in man as there are conflicting wills, there would not only have to be two natures but many more. If a man should deliberate with himself as to whether he should go to the Manichaean Center or to the theater, the Manichees will exclaim: "Notice the two natures, a good one leads here, another evil one leads away. For how explain this hesitation of the wills thwarting each other?" But I say that both wills are evil, the one that leads a man to the Manichees and the one that leads him to the theater instead. But they believe that the will by which one comes to them is good. Suppose then one of us should deliberate and through the opposition of his two wills be undecided whether he should go to the theater or to our church, will not the Manichees be troubled as to what to answer? For either they must confess, which they will not want to do, that the will which leads to our church is good just as the will is good which leads men who have received and are bound by their sacraments to their church; or else they must suppose that in one man there are two evil natures and two evil wills in conflict; and then what they are wont to say will not be true: that there is one good and one evil will. Or else they will have to be converted to the truth and no longer deny that when anyone deliberates there is just one soul pulled in different directions by different desires.

Let them no longer say, therefore, that when they perceive two conflicting wills in one man the conflict is between two opposing minds of two opposing substances, from two opposing principles, one good, the other evil. For you, O God of truth, refute them and convict them of error, as in the situation where both wills are evil when, for example, a man deliberates whether he should kill a man by poison or by the sword, whether he should seize this or that part of another man's property when he cannot seize both, whether he should squander his money on pleasure or hoard it like a miser or whether he should go to the games or to the theater if both were to be shown the same day. I add also a third possibility, whether he should rob another's house if the opportunity arose; and I add a fourth, whether he should commit adultery if the chance occurs at the same time. If all these concurred at the same moment and all were equally desired and yet cannot all be simultaneously done, then they truly tear apart the mind among four opposing wills or even more than four when one considers the variety of things which are desirable: Yet the Manichees do not hold such a multitude of different substances. So it is also with good wills. For I ask them whether it is good to take delight in reading the Apostle, and whether it is good to be delighted by the serenity of a Psalm, and good to discuss the Gospel? To each of these they will answer: "It is good." Suppose then these things all equally delight us at the same moment, are not these different wills dividing the heart of man as we deliberate which of these we should choose? All these wills are good and yet they struggle with one another until one is chosen, and then the whole will which was divided into many is unified. So also when eternity delights the higher faculties, and the pleasure of some temporal good holds the lower ones, it is the one same soul which is willing both but not either one with its whole will. And it is therefore torn apart and deeply distressed when truth gives priority to the one way and habit keeps one to the other way.

11

Thus was I heartsick and tortured, accusing myself more bitterly than usual, turning and twisting myself in my chain so that it might be totally broken, for what still held me was so small a thing. But, although small, it still held me. And you, O Lord, stood in the secret places of my soul, by a severe mercy redoubling my lashes of fear and shame, lest I should give way again and lest that small and tender tie which still remained should not be broken but renew its strength and bind me more strongly than ever before. For I was saying within myself: "Behold let it be done now, let it be done now," and with this word I came to a decision. Now I almost did it, and I did not do it; but neither did I slip back to the beginning but stood still to regain my breath. And again I tried, and I was very nearly there; I was almost touching it and grasping it, and then I was not there; I was not touching it, I was not grasping it. I hesitated to die to death and to live to life; inveterate evil had more power over me than the novelty of good; and as that very moment in which I was to become different drew nearer and nearer, it struck me with more and more horror. But I was not forced back nor turned away but held in suspense between the two.

Trifles of all trifles and vanities of vanities, my former mistresses held me back, plucking at my garment of flesh and softly murmuring: "Are you dismissing us?" and "From this moment shall we never more accompany you?" and "From this moment will you never be allowed to do this or that?" And My God, what was it, what was it they suggested in those words, "this and that?" In your mercy keep such things from the soul of your servant! How filthy, how sordid were the things they were suggesting! And now I only half heard them nor were they freely contradicting me so openly; it was as if they were muttering behind my back, stealthingly jerking my sleeve as I left so that I should turn and look at them. Yet they held me back as I delayed tearing myself away and shaking them off and taking the great step in the direction where I was called. Violence of habit said to me: "Do you think that you can live without them?" But by now it spoke very faintly. In the direction toward which I had turned my face and still trembled to take the final step, I could see the chaste dignity of Continence, serene and calm, cheerful, without wickedness, honestly entreating me to come to her without hesitating, extending her holy hands to receive and embrace me, hands full of multitudes of good examples. With her were many young men and maidens, many youths of all ages, serious widows and women grown old in virginity and in them all Continence herself, not barren but "a fruitful mother of children" (Ps 113:9), her joys by you, O Lord, her spouse. She smiled at me, and there was encouragement in her smile as though she were saying: "Can you not do what these men and women have done? Or do you think that their power is in themselves and not in the Lord their God? The Lord their God gave me to them. Why do you stand upon yourself and therefore not stand at all? Cast yourself upon Him, do not be afraid; He will not withdraw and let you fall; cast yourself fearlessly upon Him. He will receive you and heal you."

And I blushed for shame because I still heard the muttering of those vanities and still hung back hesitantly. And again it was as if she said:"Stop your ears against those unclean members of yours, so that they may be mortified. They tell you of delights, but not of such delights as the law of the Lord your God tells" (Col 3:5). This controversy raging in my heart was about nothing but myself against myself. But Alypius stayed beside me, silently waiting to see how my unusual agitation would end.

12

When from my secret depths my searching thought had dragged up and set before the sight of my heart my total misery, a storm arose within me, bringing with it a great downfall of tears. And so that I might give way to my tears I left Alypius—solitude seemed more suitable for the business of weeping—and withdrew further so that even his presence might not embarrass me. That is how I felt, and he realized it. Doubtless I had said something or other and he felt the weight of my tears in the sound of my voice, and so I left him. But he, amazed, remained there where we were sitting. I flung myself down on the ground somehow under a fig tree and gave way to tears; they streamed and flooded from my eyes, "an acceptable sacrifice to you," and I kept saying to you, perhaps not in these words but with this meaning: "And you, O Lord, how long? How long, Lord; will you be angry forever? Remember not our former iniquities" (Ps 6:3, 79:5). For I felt that they still held me fast. In misery I exclaimed: "How long, how long shall I continue to say:'tomorrow and tomorrow'? Why not now? Why not this very hour put an end to my uncleanness?"

This I said, weeping, in the most bitter contrition of my heart. And suddenly I heard a voice from a neighboring house in a singing tune saying and often repeating, in the voice of a boy or girl: "Take and read, take and read." Immediately I stopped weeping, and I began to think intently as to whether the singing of words like these was part of any children's game, and I could not remember ever hearing anything like it before. I checked the force of my tears and rose to my feet, interpreting it as nothing other than a divine command to open the book and read the first passage to be found. For I had heard of Anthony that he happened to enter when the Gospel was being read, and as though the words were spoken directly to himself he accepted the admonition: "Go, sell all that you have and give to the poor, and you shall have treasure in heaven, and come, follow me" (Mt 19:21), and by such an oracle he had been immediately converted to you.

So I eagerly returned to that place where Alypius was sitting, for there I had left the book of the Apostle when I stood up. I snatched the book opened and read in silence the passage which first met my eye: "Not in rioting and drunkenness, not in chambering and wantonness, not in strife and envying: but put you on the Lord Jesus Christ, and make not provision for the flesh in concupiscence" (Rom 13:13). I did not want to read further, there was no need to. For as soon as I reached the end of this sentence, it was as though my heart was filled with a light of confidence and all the shadows of my doubts were swept away.

Before shutting the book I put my finger on some other marker in the place; with a calm face I told Alypius what had happened. And he in turn told me what was going on in himself, which I knew nothing about. He asked to see what I had read; I showed it, and he looked further than I had read, and I was unaware of the words which followed. They were these: "Him that is weak in the faith, receive" (Rom 14:1). He applied this to himself and told me so. By this admonition he was strengthened; calmly and without hesitation he joined me in a purpose and resolution so good and so right for his character which had always been very much better than mine.

Next we go inside to mother and tell her. How she rejoices! We related to her how everything happened; she exulted and gloried and was now blessing you who are able to do above that which we ask or conceive, because she recognized that with regard to me you have given her so much more than she used to beg for when she wept so pitifully before you. For you converted me to you so that I no longer sought a wife nor any other worldly hope. I was now standing on that rule of faith just as so many years before you had shown me to her in a vision. And you had changed her mourning into joy, a joy much richer than she had wanted and much dearer and purer than she looked for by having grandchildren of my flesh.

★　　　★　　　★

BOOK TEN

24

See what a distance I have covered searching for you, O Lord, in my memory! And I have not found you outside it. Nor have I found anything about you which I did not retain in my memory from the time I first learned about you. For ever since I learned about you, I never forgot you. For wherever I found truth, there I found my God, Truth itself, and ever since I learned it, I never forgot it. And so ever since I learned of you, you have remained in my memory, and there I find you whenever I call you to mind and delight in you. These are my holy delights which you gave me in your mercy, having regard for my poverty.

25

But where do you dwell in my memory, O Lord, where do you dwell? What resting place have you fashioned for yourself? What sanctuary have you built for yourself? You have honored my memory by dwelling within it: but in what part of it do you dwell? This I am now considering. For I transcended those parts of it which the beasts also have when I was recalling you (because I did not find you there among the images of material things), and I came to those parts of it where I had stored up the affections of my mind, nor did I find you there. And I entered into the seat of my mind itself (which the mind has in memory, since the mind remembers itself) and you were not there. For just as you are not a bodily image nor an affection of any living being, such as we feel when we rejoice, sorrow, desire, fear, remember, forget, or whatever else like this we do, no, you are not the mind itself, because you are the Lord God of the mind, and all these things change, but you remain changeless over all things, and you deigned to dwell in my memory ever since I first learned of you. And why do I enquire in what place of my memory you dwell, as though there were any places at all there? Certainly you dwell in my memory, because I remember you ever since I first learned of you, and I find you there when I recall you to mind.

26

Where then did I find you so that I might learn of you? For you were not already in my memory before I learned of you. Where, then, did I find you so that I might learn of you unless in yourself above me? There is no place; we go "backward and forward" (Jb 23:8) yet there is no place. Everywhere, O Truth, you preside over all asking counsel of you and you simultaneously respond to all the diverse requests for counsel. You respond clearly, but not all hear clearly. All ask what they wish, but they do not always hear what they wish. He is your best servant who is not so eager to hear from you what he himself wills as to will what he hears from you.

27

Late have I loved you, O Beauty, so ancient and so new, late have I loved you! And behold, you were within me and I was outside, and there I sought for you, and in my deformity I rushed headlong into the well-formed things that you have made. You were with me, and I was not with you. Those outer beauties held me far from you, yet if they had not been in you, they would not have existed at all. You called, and cried out to me and broke open my deafness; you shone forth upon me and you scattered my blindness. You breathed fragrance, and I drew in my breath and I now pant for you: I tasted and I hunger and thirst; you touched me, and I burned for Your peace.

28

When I with my whole self shall cleave to you, there will no longer be for me sorrow nor labor; wholly alive will my life be, being wholly filled with you. Those whom you fill you raise up and now, since I am not yet full of you, I am a burden to myself. Pleasures of this life in which I should find sorrow conflict with the sorrows of this life in which I should rejoice, and on which side stands the victory I do not know. Woe is me, O Lord, have pity on me. My evil sorrows conflict with my good joys, and on which side stands the victory I do not know: Woe is me, O Lord, have mercy on me! Woe is me! Look, I am not concealing my wounds. You are the physician and I am ill, you are merciful, I need mercy. "Is not human life on earth a trial" (Jb 7:1)? Who wishes to have troubles and difficulties? These you order us to tolerate, not to love. No one loves what he tolerates, even though he loves to tolerate. For however greatly he rejoices in his toleration, he would yet prefer to have nothing to tolerate. In adversity I desire prosperity, in prosperity I fear adversity. What middle place is there between these two where human life is not all trial? All the prosperities of this world are caused again and again—by the fear of adversity and by the corruption of joy. And the adversities of this world are cursed once, twice, and thrice—by the desire for prosperity, by the very bitterness of adversity itself, and by the fear that it may break down our toleration. Is not then human life on earth a trial without intermission?

29

All my hope is in your great mercy. Give what you command, and command what you will. You command continence for us. And "when I knew," as it is said, "that no man can be continent, unless God gave it, this also was a part of wisdom to know whose gift it was" (Wis 8:21). Certainly it is through continence that we are brought together and returned to the One from whom we have flowed out in the many. For he loves you too little who loves anything together with you which he does not love for your sake. O love, ever burning and ever quenched! O Charity, my God, kindle me! You command continence: Give what you command and command what you will.

★   ★   ★

On the Trinity

BOOK FOURTEEN

Chapter Six

Yet so great is the power of thought that only by thinking can the mind, as it were, place itself within its own sight. Only when something is thought about is it in the mind's sight. That implies that even the mind itself, the only agent of thought, can be in its own sight only by thinking about itself. The question of how it can be understood not to be in its own sight when not thinking of itself, although it can never be separated from itself, is one I am unable to answer. Apparently, its "sight" and "itself" are two different realities—which in regard to the bodily eye is a reasonable way to speak; for whereas the eye itself has its own settled place in the body, its sight is directed to external objects and can be directed even to the stars. Nor is the eye in its own sight at all, inasmuch as it is unable to see itself unless reflected in a mirror, as we previously noted (X. 3); while nothing corresponds with that reflection when the mind by thinking of itself places itself within its own sight. When the mind is thinking of itself we can scarcely suppose that it is seeing one part of itself by another part as we see other parts of our body with one part of our body, the eye. What can be thought or said that is more absurd than this? If the mind is removed, it is removed from itself; if placed in its own sight, it is placed before itself. This means that it has changed its position from that taken when not in its own sight, as if it were removed from one place and put in another. But if it has moved in order to be seen, where does it remain in order to see? Is it doubled so that it can take two positions, one for seeing and another for being seen, in itself for seeing, before itself for being seen?

To our inquiry truth brings none of these answers; for, in fact, this mode of thinking pertains to images drawn from material objects, and it is absolutely certain that the mind is not material—at least for those few "minds" which can tell us the truth in this regard. It remains therefore, that the "sight" of the mind is essential to its nature, to which it is recalled when it thinks of itself not by a spatial movement but by an incorporeal conversion. And when not thinking of itself, although it is not within its own sight and its seeing is not defined by its nature, it nevertheless knows itself as if it were a remembrance of itself to itself. Likewise, the knowledge possessed by the expert in many sciences is present in his memory, and no part of it is in the sight of his mind unless he thinks of it, the rest being hidden in a kind of secret knowledge which is called memory.

Thus we unfolded an account of the mental trinity whereby memory provided the source from which the thinker's sight receives its form, the conformation itself being a sort of image impressed by the memory, with will or love as the agency by which the two are linked. Hence when the mind sees itself in the act of thought, it understands and knows itself, we may say that it begets this self-understanding and self-knowledge. For an immaterial object is seen when understood, and is known when it is understood. But this begetting of self-knowledge by the mind, when it sees itself as understood in thought, does not mean that previously it did not know itself. It was known as realities present in memory are known, though not thought about: as we say that a man, even when not thinking of literature but of other things, knows literature. And to these two, the begetter and the begotten, we should add the love which links them together, and this is nothing else than the will, seeking or embracing an object of enjoyment. Accordingly, we thought that a trinity was also suggested by these three names: memory, understanding, will.

Chapter Twelve

15

Now this trinity of the mind is the image of God, not because the mind remembers, understands, and loves itself, but because it also has the power to remember, understand, and love its Maker. And in doing this it attains wisdom. If it does not do this, the memory, understanding, and love of itself is no more than an act of folly. Therefore, let the mind remember its God, to whose image it was made, let it understand and love him.

In brief, let it worship the uncreated God who created it with the capacity of Himself, and in whom it can be made partaker. Hence it is written: "Behold, the worship of God is wisdom" (Jb 28:28). By participating in that supreme Light wisdom will belong to the mind not by its own light, and it will reign in bliss only where the eternal Light is. The wisdom is so called the wisdom of man as to be also that of God. If wisdom were only human it would be vain, for only God's wisdom is true wisdom. Yet when we call it God's wisdom, we do not mean the wisdom by which God is wise: He is not wise by partaking in Himself as the mind is wise by partaking in God. It is more like speaking of the justice of God not only to mean that God is just but to mean the justice He gives to man when He "justifies the ungodly" to which the Apostle alludes when speaking of those who "being ignorant of God's justice, and wanting to establish their own justice, were not subject to the justice of God" (Rom 4:5, 10:3). In this way we might speak of those who, ignorant of the wisdom of God and wanting to establish their own, were not subject to the wisdom of God.

Chapter Seventeen

23

Certainly the renewal we are discussing is not accomplished in one moment of conversion like the renewal occurring in the moment of baptism by the forgiveness of all sins, none remaining unforgiven. But it is one thing to recover from a fever, and another to regain one's health after weakness resulting from fever. It is one thing to remove a spear from the body, and another to heal the inflicted wound with treatment that follows. So to begin the cure is to remove the cause of sickness: and this occurs through the forgiveness of sins. There is in addition the healing of the sickness itself accomplished gradually by progressive renewal of the image. Both are manifest in one text of the Psalm where we read: "Who shows mercy upon all your iniquities," which occurs in baptism, and then: "Who heals all your sicknesses" (Ps 103:3), which refers to daily advances whereby the image is renewed. The Apostle spoke of this in clear words: "If our outer man decays, yet is our inner man renewed from day to day" (2 Cor 4:16)—but he is "renewed" as he said in the previously quoted texts, "in the knowledge of God," that is, "in justice and holiness of truth." He who is thus renewed by daily progressing in the knowledge of God, in justice and holiness of truth, is converting the direction of his love from the temporal to the eternal, from visible to intelligible things, from carnal to spiritual things, trying assiduously to control and reduce all desire for the former and to bind himself by love to the latter. All his success in this depends on divine assistance, for it is God's word that "without me you can do nothing" (Jn 15:5).

When the final day of life reveals a man, in the midst of this progress and growth, holding steadfast to the faith of the Mediator, the holy angels will await him to bring him home to the God whom he has served and by whom he must be perfected; and at the end of the world he will receive an incorruptible body, not for punishment but for glory. For the likeness of God will be perfect in this image only in the perfect vision of God: of which vision the Apostle Paul says: "Now we see through a glass darkly, but then face-to-face" (1 Cor 13:12). And again: "But we with unveiled face beholding the glory of the Lord are transformed into the same image from glory to glory, as from the spirit of the Lord" (2 Cor 3:18). This describes the daily process in those progressing as they should.

Chapter Eighteen

24

  This statement is from the Apostle John: "Beloved, we are now the children of God, and it has not yet appeared what we shall be: but we know that when He appears we shall be like Him, for we shall see Him as he is" (Jn 3:2). This indicates that the full likeness of God is attained in His image only when it has attained the full vision of Him. John's words may indeed be considered as referring to the body's immortality; for also in that we shall be like God, but only like the Son, since He alone in the trinity took a body in which He died, rose again, and which He bore with Him into heaven. We may also speak here of an image of the Son of God in which we, like Him, shall have an immortal body, conformed in that respect to the image of the Son only, not of the Father nor of the Holy Spirit. For of Him alone do we read and receive with very sound faith that "the Word was made flesh" (Jn 1:14). So the Apostle says: "Whom He foreknew, them He also predestined to be conformed to the image of His Son, that He might be firstborn among many brethren" (Rom 8:29). "Firstborn," in fact, "of the dead," in the words of the same Apostle (Col 1:18)—that death whereby His flesh was sown in dishonor and rose again in glory (1 Cor 15:43). According to this image of the Son, to which we are conformed through immortality in the body, we likewise do that which the same Paul says elsewhere: "As we have borne the image of the earthly, let us also bear the image of Him who is from heaven" (1 Cor 15:49). This means: Let us who were mortal according to Adam believe with true faith and sure and steadfast hope that we shall be immortal according to Christ through faith, not yet in reality but in hope. Indeed in this context the Apostle was speaking of the resurrection of the body.

Chapter Nineteen

25

But if we consider that image of which it is written: "Let us make man in our image and likeness" (Gn 1:26), not "in my image" or "in your image," we must believe that man was made in the image of the Trinity; and we have devoted our best efforts to discover and understand this. Therefore in respect to this image we may better interpret John's words: "We shall be like Him, for we shall see Him as He is!" Here the Apostle is speaking of Him of whom he has said: "We are the children of God!"

The immortality of the flesh, moreover, will be made perfect in the moment of resurrection which, as Paul says, will be "in the twinkling of an eye, at the last trumpet: and the dead shall be raised uncorrupted, and we shall be changed" (1 Cor 15:52). For in the twinkling of an eye there shall rise again before the judgment that spiritual body in strength, incorruption, and glory which now as a natural body is being sown in weakness, corruption, and dishonor. But the image that is being renewed day by day in the spirit of the mind, and in the knowledge of God, not outwardly but inwardly, will be perfected by that vision which shall exist after the judgment as face-to-face—the vision which now is only developing, through a glass darkly (1 Cor 13:12).

We ought to understand the perfecting of the image by these words: "We shall be like Him, for we shall see Him as He is." This is the gift to be given us then when we hear the call: "Come you blessed of my Father, possess the kingdom prepared for you" (Mt 25:34). Then the godless one shall be removed so that he does not see the glory of the Lord, when those on the left hand go into eternal punishment, and those on the right hand into eternal life. But as the Truth has told us, "This is eternal life, that they may know you the one true God, and Jesus Christ whom you have sent" (Jn 17:3).

This wisdom of contemplation is, I believe, in its strict sense, distinguished in Holy Scripture from knowledge, and called wisdom—a human wisdom, yet coming to man only from God: participating in whom, the reasonable and intellectual mind is able to become wise in truth. At the end of his dialogue *Hortensius*, we see Cicero praising this contemplative wisdom. "If," he says, "we meditate day and night, if we sharpen our understanding which is the mind's eye and take care that it may not grow dull, if, that is, we live the life of philosophy, then we may have good hope that although our power of feeling and thinking is mortal and transient, it will be pleasant for us to pass away when life's duties are done. Nor will our death be offensive to us but a repose from living, and if, however, as the greatest and most famous of the ancient philosophers have believed, our souls are eternal and divine, then we may rightly suppose that the more constant a soul has been in following its own course, that is, in the use of reason and zeal in inquiry, and the less it has mingled and involved itself in the vices and delusions of man, so much the easier will be its ascent and return to its heavenly country." Afterward, he adds this final statement to summarize and conclude his discussion: "Therefore, to end this long discourse, after these pursuits have filled our life, if it is our will to pass quietly into nothingness or to go immediately from our present home to another far better one, we should dedicate all our energy and attention to these studies."

I cannot but wonder that so powerful a mind should offer to men who live the life of philosophy, the life-giving happiness in the contemplation of truth, a "pleasant passing away" when human life's duties are done, if our power of thinking and feeling is mortal and transient; as though this would be the death and destruction of that which we so little loved or so fiercely hated that its passing away would be pleasant to us. He did not learn that from the philosophers to whom he gives such great praise; his opinion smacked rather of the New Academy, which had led him to skepticism even about the most evident truths. But, as he admits, the tradition that came to him from those philosophers who were the greatest and most famous was that souls are eternal. Indeed, the advice is appropriate for eternal souls so that they may be found at the end of their life "following their own course, that is, in the use of reason and the zeal in inquiry," not "mingling and involving themselves in the vices and delusions of men," so that they may more easily return to God. But for unhappy men, as all men must be whose mortality is supported by reason alone without faith in the Mediator, this course which consists in the love of God and in the search for truth is not enough. I have done my best to demonstrate this in previous books of this treatise, especially the fourth and thirteenth.

Chapter 3

TALKING ABOUT GOD AND GENDER:

JULIAN OF NORWICH

Julian of Norwich lived during the late fourteenth century in England. Unlike the other figures discussed in this book, we know little about her life—even the exact dates of her birth and death are a mystery. Her writing, however, has a contemporary quality that has made her increasingly popular during the last century and our own. Her message is that God is known to us in an embodied form that is apprehended by all of our senses. God is providentially working all things for good so that we can trust that all shall be well.

Most notably, Julian broke out of the standard masculine metaphors when speaking about God. She talked of Christ as a masculine, young lover, to be sure. But she also described God as our Mother.

There are few issues that have had so revolutionary an effect on our everyday lives as the rethinking of the role of women in society. We are all familiar with the claims of feminism, whether on the job or in the classroom. Our language itself has felt the effects of this change in the way many think. Language changes. It evolves, grows, shrinks, as it has to in order to do its job of conveying meaning. In English today, our understanding of gender has changed. We cannot simply use gender-specific words and expect that people will understand them to refer to both sexes. So talk of "God and man" must give way to "God and persons," or "God and human beings," or some such thing. Beyond that there is the more serious issue of how sexuality influences our conception of language. When we speak of God as "He," does that connote a certain meaning that we associate with human males? More subtly, does our very concept of God, if spoken of in masculine terms, leave out aspects of divinity that are better understood in feminine terms? From that we must also ask, does referring to God in words of one gender exclude those of the opposite sex? Can we find ways to be more inclusive in our language—not for the sake of playground games—but because doing so is the only way to expand our understanding of the realities we are attempting to express with language?

Many women have felt excluded by the political structures of certain religious groups that have restricted their participation to certain functions. Some of them, given the heightened consciousness that feminism has created, now find language which is not gender-inclusive offensive, because it signals for them a larger exclusiveness, the pain of which is acute. So the task of rethinking how we conceive of God and gender is very real and carries with it a certain urgency. Theologian Rosemary Ruether thinks that metaphors about the masculinity of God are taken too seriously by Christians. The first commandment's prohibition against making a graven image of God should also be extended to verbal images, she argues. Thinking of God exclusively as a "he" is idolatrous. Ruether argues that we must use gender-inclusive language to properly represent God.

Some like Ruether take the claim about inclusiveness further, holding that the metaphor of God as Father and us as God's children breeds a kind of spiritual infantilism that should be rejected along with the masculine God imagery. Even more radical is the thought of Mary Daly, whose distress over matters of gender led her out of the Catholic Church into witchcraft. For her any talk about God as masculine is unacceptable, because God is, like the Earth, paradigmatically feminine. She presents a dualistic image of God, whereby evil is associated with masculinity, and the Trinity is completely rejected as an apt representation of divinity.

Many would find this talk extreme and see little value in simply replacing a male-oriented imagery with a female. Actually feminism of the Ruether-Daly type is heretical, departing from the living tradition of the church, dating back to the apostles. It does little to enhance human dignity and introduces enmity into the heart of life. Others point to non-Christian traditions that contain less gender-specific images of God than the Christian Trinity. Abdal Hakim Murad, for example, suggests that in Islam God is not gendered. God is *Allah,* but never "Father." The masculine pronoun is used for Allah, but it is not allegoric, since it is common in Arabic for nouns that in English would be neuter to be masculine, because there is no neuter form in the language. No male preference is implied by referring to Allah as he, anymore than one is implied by the common practice of using the feminine for what would in English be neuter plurals. Murad insists that the imagery of God is not male or female but based on an image that contains both: the Ninety-Nine Names. The Names of Majesty include Allah the Powerful, the Overwhelming, the Judge—all masculine ideas. The Names of Beauty include Allah the All-Compassionate, the Mild, the Loving-kind—all feminine.

When it comes to the Christian tradition, there are examples of meditations on the names of God. Luis de Léon, writing in Spain in the sixteenth century, consciously appropriates the Moslem meditation on the names of God. He mentions fourteen names. Most have a masculine connotation: Shepherd, Everlasting Father, King, Prince, Husband, Son. But at least two suggest the feminine: Bud and Beloved. Yet Luis de Léon's overall frame of reference is Trinitarian to be sure, with an element of neoplatonism added, which reinforces the masculine imagery.

There are few efforts to present feminine imagery that are as developed, and hence as valuable to the contemporary discussion, as Julian's. Without abandoning the traditional Christian images of God, she adds a gender-inclusive dimension to her God talk. It is to her thought we now turn.

JULIAN'S LIFE AND TIMES

Julian lived during the late Middle Ages in a time of great transition. Christian Europe's efforts at expansion that marked the Crusades of the High Middle Ages met new resistance from fierce Moslem counterattacks in North Africa and Granada, setting the scene for the ascent of the Ottoman Empire. The Christian East, though badly battered, was able to maintain a large degree of independence from the Latin West. The hostilities that Christians had directed against the Moslems in an earlier age now were turning upon themselves. England invaded France and began the Hundred Years' War, and Central European powers battled against the Hohenstaufen.

Social tensions among ethnic groups and economic classes also worsened. A new wave of intolerance of non-Christians marked the time and saw the expulsion of Jews and Muslims from many areas. Tensions flared among Christians as well. In the countryside constant battles raged over ownership of the land and the status of citizens as free or bound to a prince. In the cities workers' guilds had obtained a large measure of political power and freedom for their members. But inevitably power struggles developed, as was the case with the Ciompi revolt in 1378 in Florence, when the tight grip of a few guilds and families elicited the rebellion of those being pushed aside.

Nature as well was not kind to the age of Julian. Food production was reduced by a worsening of the weather. Overcrowding was common in many cities, where fierce outbreaks of diseases like the black plague killed thousands.

The church of the time was likewise rocked by strife, best illustrated by the Great Schism. The battle between the papacy and the princes of Europe for temporal power was a constant drama of medieval society. That struggle had led to the relocation of the papacy from Rome to the city of Avignon from 1309 to 1377, where it came under the strong influence of the French kings. In 1378, a rival pope was elected in Rome and a period began in which there were two men, one in Avignon and the other in Rome, each claiming to be the valid successor of St. Peter and each enjoying the support of powerful political forces. The Schism marked the defeat of the papacy's attempt to exert political control over the kings of Europe and a new independence of the civil power from the ecclesiastical.

Such disruption of the religious landscape opened the way for what can be described as independence movements within the church. Just as princes felt a new freedom from Roman influence, so individuals felt a new liberty to experiment with their own religious sensibilities without the need for church approval. One such person was Julian's English contemporary, John Wycliff. An Oxford-educated clergyman, Wycliff professed that the church could not make an absolute claim to secular power, especially if church leaders were not exercising their responsibilities in the spirit of the Gospel. This idea was music to the ears of English princes like John of Gaunt, the Duke of Lancaster, who granted Wycliff protection against the rebukes of Pope Gregory XI.

Wycliff went on to expand his views to matters of the spiritual life. He argued that the papacy did not have power over the lives of individuals. He stressed that Scripture, not the pope, was the standard of faith and highest authority for every Christian.

His views gave rise to a movement of laypeople known as the Lollards. These "poor priests," as they were known, traveled throughout England and western Europe, preaching devotion to Scripture and to a sincere and simple life of faith.

In this context the life of Julian can begin to be understood. She described herself as an "ignorant woman," by which she meant that she did not have the advantage of a university education and was not learned in philosophy and theology. She lived as an anchoress at the church in Norwich. As such she was consigned, of her own free will, to spend her life in a small apartment adjacent to the church, where she lived alone with her cats. Her primary contact with the outside world came through a window that opened out onto the street. Through that window she would meet with passersby seeking advice from a holy woman. Her unusual lifestyle was understood by all as a form of consecration to God, for her entrance into this life had been a public event. The bishop of the town along with a crowd of the faithful had held a public service in which she was sealed into her apartment, there to spend the rest of her days in prayer and in counseling the spiritually hungry. Traditionally this was something done by a mature woman, whose need for mobility naturally had decreased with age. It was a dignified and honored way for a woman of special spiritual gifts to live the last part of her life. Just as in the Hindu *Code of Manu* the old man who has walked in the way of holiness spends the last part of his life as a wandering holy man, freed from the responsibilities of being a householder, so too the anchoress was given a role by her society for which she was by disposition suited.

There was a darker side to the life of an anchoress as well. Given the social restrictions on women, a woman religious with an independent cast was faced with the dilemma of either living under the highly regulated regimens of the convent, which presupposed a subservient role for each of its inhabitants, or to leave in disgrace and return to her family, unable to ever marry or have an independent existence outside of the home of a male family member, who would certainly not simply allow her to spend her time any way she liked but would press her into the economic work of the household, thus placing her in a position not very different from the convent.

JULIAN'S *SHOWINGS*

We know so little about Julian's life and the motivations that caused her to become an anchoress that we must look at the broad historical context and at the text of her sole surviving writing to learn more about her. *Showings* was begun sometime after May 13, 1373, the date that she gives in the book as the day when she received her first vision at the age of thirty. We really do not know how much later, because there are few ways to corroborate her account. Julian clearly was not a widely known figure in her day, nor was she someone whose writings have had a profound effect on subsequent genera- tions. It was not until 1670 that the Englishman Serenus Casey pub- lished a version of her work. It is largely in our own century that interest in Julian has increased, begun no doubt by the British Museum's purchase of a manuscript of the short text at the beginning of the century. It was not until 1977 that a complete critical edition of *Showings* was completed by Edmond College and James Walsh.

Showings is, in Julian's words, "a vision shown by the goodness of God to a devout woman…in which are very many words of comfort, greatly moving for all those who desire to be Christ's lovers." Herein is contained a presentation of two of the three most remarkable themes in her book: an optimistic faith that all shall be well and an embodied sense of the courteous love of God. To those is added the third, and most timely: Julian's perception of the motherhood of God.

From the start, there is an odd incongruity in the style of the work. Amid the pious and humbly self-effacing statements about her "ignorance" are found numerous elements, especially in the long text, that are clearly not the products of an uneducated woman recluse who had a vision. So far different is the style of this piece from the rambling, eccentric, confused musing of her contemporary Margery Kempe that one is forced to conclude that either Julian did not write all of her book, or her pious diminutives about her lack of learning are nothing more than a literary convention. We read, for instance, of God, the blessed Trinity, who is "everlasting being, just as he is eternal and without beginning." Or of virtues which "we have received from our substance, given to us in nature." Or of human nature that has been "created from nothing." Such language is that of the Schoolmen, the learned theologians of Julian's day who were grounded in the language of Scholasticism. Was Julian edited by a theologian to embellish her own visions and add to them sophistication and doctrinal correctness that saved them from the egregious errors of Margery Kempe or the Lollards? It is not at all unlikely. In fact, it is entirely more likely to conclude that than to think that Julian, as a woman recluse, somehow attained that learning on her own. Given that, it is difficult to speak about Julian as a woman's voice without taking into consideration the likelihood of editorship or "false" identity and the dynamics of the culture that made those a necessity.

Julian's Message

THE MOTHERHOOD OF GOD

We can, nevertheless, hear the message of *Showings,* at least in its simplest sense, and learn about the issues with which it grapples. Reading Julian in the long text, we are treated repeatedly to her references to the motherhood of God. Julian was not alone in attributing qualities of motherhood to God. We read in Isaiah: "Like a son is comforted by his mother, so will I comfort you." We can also look to the church father St. Irenaeus, who constantly referred to the Holy Spirit as feminine. Julian's contemporaries, St. Bridget of Sweden and St. Catherine of Sienna, also refer to the feminine aspects of God.

A long tradition exists in Judaism, Islam, and Christianity discussing the attributes of God. In Islam, in the writings of an Ibn Arabi, or in Christianity, in the work of Pseudo-Dionysius or Luis de León, that discussion took the form of meditations on the names of God. Some of those names could clearly convey motherly attributes. In Judaism, in addition to the use of the feminine *ruach adonai* (the spirit of the Lord) there is the discussion of the *Shekhinah*—a feminine aspect of the one God—that is part of the early Kabbalah tradition.

Although Julian did not invent the theme, she did express it with a beauty and a vigor that is perhaps her greatest legacy to us. In her language, God is both Mother and Father. She emphasizes the complementarity of the roles: "I am he, the power and goodness of fatherhood: I am she, the wisdom and lovingness of motherhood." And above all, "I am the unity."

This feminine dimension of God is more than a poetic flourish; it is a clearly thought out attempt to find imagery for God that reflects the fullness and the ultimate unity of all that is. Julian, as a woman, could not simply think of God as a he. At the same time, Julian, as a profound thinker, could not simply stop with the use of feminine words to describe God. She was beyond ideological slogans in her statement: "as truly as God is our Father, so truly is God our Mother."

Her concern was to present God in a way that reflected the relational character of the Godhead. Perhaps from William of St. Thierry or some other font flowing within the Augustinian tradition, Julian takes the idea of God as Trinity: as three persons who relate to one another in a community of love and, in the process, manifest the fullness of God and present a type for all human relationships. She writes:

> Our great Father, almighty God, who is being, knows us and loved us before time began. Out of this knowledge, in his most wonderful deep love, by the prescient eternal counsel of all the blessed Trinity, he wanted the second person to become our Mother, our brother and our savior. (296)

Jesus as both mother and brother; Jesus as androgynous, not sexless, but comprehensive in his incarnated, embodied being is further developed:

> And so Jesus is our true Mother in nature by our first creation, and he is our true Mother in grace by his taking our created nature. All the lovely works and all the sweet loving offices of beloved motherhood are appropriated to the second person.... (296)

Julian then goes on to speak of three ways of contemplating motherhood in God. The first is what she calls "the foundation of our nature's creation," or simply, our Mother in nature. Here she speaks of Jesus as the one who gives us our life in the sense of creating us. Jesus does this like a mother whose service is nearest, readiest, and surest, most natural, most loving, and truest.

Not only does Jesus create us, but also in the incarnation, he has taken on our human form and borne our weaknesses. This is the second way in which Julien contemplates motherhood in God. She realized this in one of her early visions: "I saw a great unity between Christ and us; for when he was in pain we were in pain, and all creatures able to suffer pain suffered with him" (141–42). Thus Christ carries us, as a mother does her unborn child, close to her heart, within her, united with her. This second way is a way of grace, a way by which the grace of God penetrates all things and by which all things are brought back to God through Christ, their Mother.

The third way is the motherhood of God at work. Like a mother, Christ illumines our understanding so that we can see the folly of straying from God. He comforts us like a gracious mother. Like a mother he does this with humility and meekness. Likewise, as our earthly mother could not stand to see her child perish, so Christ would do everything, even give his life, for the well-being of his child.

THE COURTESY OF CHRIST

Out of this sense of Christ as mother comes another image, which works not in any sense to contradict, but rather to complement that of motherhood. In this vision, Julian sees Christ as a man, in fact, he is a courtier. A courtier in Julian's day was a gentleman, a man of virtue, of honor, of romance, and of love. Julian's perception of Jesus is nothing less than sensual in her vision of the true man: "a handsome person and tall, honorable, the greatest lord, splendidly clad in honors. He sits erect." What a vividly descriptive image, not of an abstract essence, not of a Platonic form, not of an insipid, pious man-child, but of a real, good-looking, virile man.

Julian is madly in love with this man and she makes no secret of it. At one point, she has a vision of Christ appearing to her "courteous, joyful" and saying to her: "I am he whom you love. I am he in whom you delight. I am he whom you serve. I am he for whom you long. I am he whom you desire" (147).

This sensuous picture of Christ is repeated when Julian contemplates, to her great consternation, the suffering of Christ. Again, we do not get a treatise on the juridical theory of the atonement or a discourse on the justice of God. Rather we are told that she sees the face of Jesus as he is suffering. She focuses on his lips, his eyes. She sees the life ebbing from his lovely face.

Not only does she envision Christ in bodily form, she experiences him in her body. She sums up her visions in the beginning of the short text of *Showings* by speaking of three graces she received from God. The first is to have an understanding of Christ's passion, which she experiences in the manner just discussed. The second is to have a bodily sickness. The third is to have three wounds. In each case the language of perception is physical: a vision of the lovely Christ's face dying, a sickness in her body, a wound in her body. Repeatedly she refers to having "bodily sight" of these things. She speaks of "feeling as a touch" the presence of God. All the imagery is tactile, earthly, human.

The similarity to the Franciscan tradition of devotion to the humanity of Christ is evident. But whether there is a direct influence is not clear. It is entirely likely that such an understanding came not from reading Francis or Bonaventure but from her own womanly experience. Likewise for the similarity with the courtly love tradition found in Bernard of Clairvaux and also in Dante. Love, courtly love, applied to her lover Christ is her own embodied, impassioned response to God. That is what gives Julian a voice that is her own, a poetry that even the scholastic glosses added perhaps by a pious editor cannot erase, and in the end, a relevance for us who as embodied, sexual, sensual women and men, must seek God.

In the final analysis, Julian's message is one of profound optimism. Surrounded by a strife-torn society, she saw in her visions a God, who like a Mother, was gathering all her children to herself. And who like a courtly, lovely, strong prince would keep them from evil. Through the working of the Trinity creating, redeeming, and sustaining us, all things in the end are destined to fulfill God's purposes. Julian's sense of the sweetness of God, a sweetness she touched and tasted, brings with it a confidence and peace in God's loving care. In her own memorable words: "And so our good Lord answered all the questions and doubts which I could raise, saying most comfortingly in this fashion: I will make all things well, I shall make all things well, I may make all things well and I can make all things well; and you will see yourself, that all things will be well" (151).

BIBLIOGRAPHY

Hudleston, Roger. *Revelations of Divine Love.* London, 1927.

Walsh, James. *The Revelations of Julian of Norwich.* London, 1961.

Walsh, James, and Edmund Colledge. *Julian of Norwich: Showings.* The Classics of Western Spirituality. New York: Paulist Press, 1978.

Wolters, Clifford. *Julian of Norwich: Revelations of Divine Love.* Harmondsworth, 1966.

SHOWINGS,
THE SHORT TEXT[4]

CHAPTER XV

And so our good Lord answered to all the questions and doubts which I could raise, saying most comfortingly in this fashion: I will make all things well, I shall make all things well, I may make all things well and I can make all things well; and you will see that yourself, that all things will be well. When he says that he 'may', I understand this to apply to the Father; and when he says that he 'can', I understand this for the Son; and when he says 'I will', I understand this for the Holy Spirit; and when he says 'I shall', I understand this for the unity of the blessed Trinity, three persons in one truth; and when he says 'You will see yourself', I understand this for the union of all men who will be saved in the blessed Trinity.

And in these five words God wishes to be enclosed in rest and in peace. And so Christ's spiritual thirst has an end. For his spiritual thirst is his longing in love, and that persists and always will until we see him on the day of judgment; for we who shall be saved and shall be Christ's joy and bliss are still here, and shall be until that day. Therefore his thirst is this incompleteness of his joy, that he does not now possess us in himself as wholly as he then will.

All this was shown to me as a revelation of his compassion, for on the day of judgment it will cease. So he has pity and compassion on us and he longs to possess us, but his wisdom and his love do not permit the end to come until the best time. And in these same five words said before: 'I may make all things well', I understand powerful consolation from all the deeds of our Lord

---

4. *Julian of Norwich: Showings,* Trans. Edmund Colledge and James Walsh, the Classics of Western Spirituality (New York/Mahwah, N.J.: Paulist Press, 1978).

which are still to be performed; for just as the blessed Trinity created everything from nothing, just so the same blessed Trinity will make well all things which are not well. It is God's will that we pay great heed to all the deeds which he has performed, for he wishes us to know from them all which he will do; and he revealed that to me by those words which he said: And you will see yourself that every kind of thing will be well. I understand this in two ways: One is that I am well content that I do not know it. It is God's will that we should know in general that all will be well, but it is not God's will that we should know it now except as it applies to us for the present, and that is the teaching of Holy Church.

CHAPTER XVI

God showed me the very great delight that he has in all men and women who accept, firmly and humbly and reverently, the preaching and teaching of Holy Church, for he is Holy Church. For he is the foundation, he is the substance, he is the teaching, he is the teacher, he is the end, he is the reward for which every faithful soul labours; and he is known and will be known to every soul to whom the Holy Spirit declares this. And I am certain that all who seek in this way will prosper, for they are seeking God.

All this which I have now said and more which I shall presently say is solace against sin; for when I first saw that God does everything which is done, I did not see sin, and then I saw that all is well. But when God did show me sin, it was then that he said: All will be well.

And when almighty God had shown me his goodness so plenteously and fully, I wished to know, concerning a certain person whom I loved, what her future would be; and by wishing this I impeded myself, for I was not then told this. And then I was answered in my reason, as it were by a friendly man: Accept it generally, and contemplate the courtesy of your Lord God as he reveals it to you, for it is more honour to God to contemplate him in all things than in any one special thing. I agreed, and with that I learned that it is more honour to God to know everything in general than it is to take delight in any special thing. And if I were to act wisely, in accordance with this teaching, I should not be glad because of any special thing or be distressed by anything at all, for all will be well.

God brought to my mind that I should sin; and because of the delight that I had in contemplating him, I did not at once pay attention to this revelation. And our Lord very courteously waited until I was ready to attend, and then our Lord brought to my mind, along with my sins, the sins of all my fellow Christians, all in general and none in particular.

THE FIFTY-EIGHTH CHAPTER

God the blessed Trinity, who is everlasting being, just as he is eternal from without beginning, just so was it in his eternal purpose to create human nature, which fair nature was first prepared for his own Son, the second person; and when he wished, by full agreement of the whole Trinity he created us all once. And in our creating he joined and united us to himself, and through this union we are kept as pure and as noble as we were created. By the power of that same precious union we love our Creator and delight in him, praise him and thank him and endlessly rejoice in him. And this is the work which is constantly performed in every soul which will be saved, and this is the godly will mentioned before.

And so in our making, God almighty is our loving Father, and God all wisdom is our loving Mother, with the love and the goodness of the Holy Spirit, which is all one God, one Lord. And in the joining and the union he is our very true spouse and we his beloved wife and his fair maiden, with which wife he was never displeased; for he says: I love you and you love me, and our love will never divide in two.

I contemplated the work of all the blessed Trinity, in which contemplation I saw and understood these three properties: the property of the fatherhood, and the property of the motherhood, and the property of the lordship in one God. In our almighty Father we have our protection and our bliss, as regards our natural substance, which is ours by our creation from without beginning; and in the second person, in knowledge and wisdom we have our perfection, as regards our sensuality, our restoration and our salvation, for he is our Mother, brother and saviour; and in our good

Lord the Holy Spirit we have our reward and our gift for our living and our labour, endlessly surpassing all that we desire in his marvellous courtesy, out of his great plentiful grace. For all our life consists of three: In the first we have our being, and in the second we have our increasing, and in the third we have our fulfillment. The first is nature, the second is mercy, the third is grace.

As to the first, I saw and understood that the high might of the Trinity is our Father, and the deep wisdom of the Trinity is our Mother, and the great love of the Trinity is our Lord; and all these we have in nature and in our substantial creation. And furthermore I saw that the second person, who is our Mother, substantially the same beloved person, has now become our mother sensually, because we are double by God's creating, that is to say substantial and sensual. Our substance is the higher part, which we have in our Father, God almighty; and the second person of the Trinity is our Mother in nature in our substantial creation, in whom we are founded and rooted, and he is our Mother of mercy in taking our sensuality. And so our Mother is working on us in various ways, in whom our parts are kept undivided; for in our Mother Christ we profit and increase, and in mercy he reforms and restores us, and by the power of his Passion, his death and his Resurrection he unites us to our substance. So our Mother works in mercy on all his beloved children who are docile and obedient to him, and grace works with mercy, and especially in two properties, as it was shown, which working belongs to the third person, the Holy Spirit. He works, rewarding and giving. Rewarding is a gift for our confidence which the Lord makes to those who have laboured; and giving is a courteous act which he does freely, by grace, fulfilling and surpassing all that creatures deserve.

Thus in our Father, God almighty, we have our being, and in our Mother of mercy we have our reforming and our restoring, in whom our parts are united and all made perfect man, and through the rewards and the gifts of grace of the Holy Spirit we are fulfilled. And our substance is in our Father, God almighty, and our substance is in our Mother, God all wisdom, and our substance is in our Lord God, the Holy Spirit, all goodness, for our substance is whole in each person of the Trinity, who is one God. And our sensuality is only in the second person, Christ Jesus, in whom is the Father and the Holy Spirit; and in him and by him we are powerfully taken out of hell and out of the wretchedness on earth, and gloriously brought up into heaven, and blessedly united to our substance, increased in riches and nobility by all the power of Christ and by the grace and operation of the Holy Spirit.

THE FIFTY-NINTH CHAPTER

And we have all this bliss by mercy and grace, and this kind of bliss we never could have had and known, unless that property of goodness which is in God had been opposed, through which we have this bliss. For wickedness has been suffered to rise in opposition to that goodness; and the goodness of mercy and grace opposed that wickedness, and turned everything to goodness and honour for all who will be saved. For this is that property in God which opposed good to evil. So Jesus Christ, who opposes good to evil, is our true Mother. We have our being from him, where the foundation of motherhood begins, with all the sweet protection of love which endlessly follows.

As truly as God is our Father, so truly is God our Mother, and he revealed that in everything, and especially in these sweet words where he says: I am he; that is to say: I am he, the power and goodness of fatherhood; I am he, the wisdom and the lovingness of motherhood; I am he, the light and the grace which is all blessed love; I am he, the Trinity; I am he, the unity; I am he, the great supreme goodness of every kind of thing; I am he who makes you to love; I am he who makes you to long; I am he, the endless fulfilling of all true desires. For where the soul is highest, noblest, most honourable, still it is lowest, meekest and mildest.

And from this foundation in substance we have all the powers of our sensuality by the gift of nature, and by the help and the furthering of mercy and grace, without which we cannot profit. Our great

Father, almighty God, who is being, knows us and loved us before
time began. Out of this knowledge, in his most wonderful deep love,
by the prescient eternal counsel of all the blessed Trinity, he wanted
the second person to become our Mother, our brother and our saviour. From this it follows that as truly as God is our Father, so truly is
God our Mother. Our Father wills, our Mother works, our good
Lord the Holy Spirit confirms. And therefore it is our part to love
our God in whom we have our being, reverently thanking and praising him for our creation, mightily praying to our Mother for mercy
and pity, and to our Lord the Holy Spirit for help and grace. For in
these three is all our life: nature, mercy and grace, of which we have
mildness, patience and pity, and hatred of sin and wickedness; for the
virtues must of themselves hate sin and wickedness.

And so Jesus is our true Mother in nature by our first creation, and he is our true Mother in grace by his taking our created
nature. All the lovely works and all the sweet loving offices of
beloved motherhood are appropriated to the second person, for in
him we have this godly will, whole and safe forever, both in nature
and in grace, from his own goodness proper to him.

I understand three ways of contemplating motherhood in
God. The first is the foundation of our nature's creation; the second
is his taking of our nature, where the motherhood of grace begins;
the third is the motherhood at work. And in that, by the same
grace, everything is penetrated, in length and in breadth, in height
and in depth without end; and it is all one love.

THE SIXTIETH CHAPTER

But now I should say a little more about this penetration, as I
understood our Lord to mean: How we are brought back by the
motherhood of mercy and grace into our natural place, in which
we were created by the motherhood of love, a mother's love which
never leaves us.

Our Mother in nature, our Mother in grace, because he
wanted altogether to become our Mother in all things, made the

foundation of his work most humbly and most mildly in the maiden's womb. And he revealed that in the first revelation, when he brought that meek maiden before the eye of my understanding in the simple stature which she had when she conceived; that is to say that our great God, the supreme wisdom of all things, arrayed and prepared himself in this humble place, all ready in our poor flesh, himself to do the service and the office of motherhood in everything. The mother's service is nearest, readiest and surest: nearest because it is most natural, readiest because it is most loving, and surest because it is truest. No one ever might or could perform this office fully, except only him. We know that all our mothers bear us for pain and for death. O, what is that? But our true Mother Jesus, he alone bears us for joy and for endless life, blessed may he be. So he carries us within him in love and travail, until the full time when he wanted to suffer the sharpest thorns and cruel pains that ever were or will be, and at the last he died. And when he had finished, and had borne us so for bliss, still all this could not satisfy his wonderful love. And he revealed this in these great surpassing words of love. If I could suffer more, I would suffer more. He could not die any more, but he did not want to cease working; therefore he must needs nourish us, for the precious love of motherhood has made him our debtor.

The mother can give her child to suck of her milk, but our precious Mother Jesus can feed us with himself, and does, most courteously and most tenderly, with the blessed sacrament, which is the precious food of true life; and with all the sweet sacraments he sustains us most mercifully and graciously, and so he meant in these blessed words, where he said: I am he whom Holy Church preaches and teaches to you. That is to say: All the health and the life of the sacraments, all the power and the grace of my word, all the goodness which is ordained in Holy Church for you, I am he.

The mother can lay her child tenderly to her breast, but our tender Mother Jesus can lead us easily into his blessed breast through his sweet open side, and show us there a part of the godhead and of the joys of heaven, with inner certainty of endless bliss.

And that he revealed in the tenth revelation, giving us the same understanding in these sweet words which he says: See, how I love you, looking into his blessed side, rejoicing.

This fair lovely word 'mother' is so sweet and so kind in itself that it cannot truly be said of anyone or to anyone except of him and to him who is the true Mother of life and of all things. To the property of motherhood belong nature, love, wisdom and knowledge, and this is God. For though it may be so that our bodily bringing to birth is only little, humble and simple in comparison with our spiritual bringing to birth, still it is he who does it in the creatures by whom it is done. The kind, loving mother who knows and sees the need of her child guards it very tenderly, as the nature and condition of motherhood will have. And always as the child grows in age and in stature, she acts differently, but she does not change her love. And when it is even older, she allows it to be chastised to destroy its faults, so as to make the child receive virtues and grace. This work, with everything which is lovely and good, our Lord performs in those by whom it is done. So he is our Mother in nature by the operation of grace in the lower part, for love of the higher part. And he wants us to know it, for he wants to have all our love attached to him; and in this I saw that every debt which we owe by God's command to fatherhood and motherhood is fulfilled in truly loving God, which blessed love Christ works in us. And this was revealed in everything, and especially in the great bounteous words when he says: I am he whom you love.

THE SIXTY-FIRST CHAPTER

And in our spiritual bringing to birth he uses more tenderness, without any comparison, in protecting us. By so much as our soul is more precious in his sight, he kindles our understanding, he prepares our ways, he eases our conscience, he comforts our soul, he illumines our heart and gives us partial knowledge and love of his blessed divinity, with gracious memory of his sweet humanity and his blessed Passion, with courteous wonder over his great surpassing goodness, and makes us to love everything which he loves for love of him, and to be well satisfied with him and with all his works. And when we fall, quickly he raises us up with his loving embrace and his gracious touch. And when we are strengthened by his sweet working, then we willingly choose him by his grace, that we shall be his servants and his lovers, constantly and forever.

And yet after this he allows some of us to fall more heavily and more grievously than ever we did before, as it seems to us. And then we who are not all wise think that everything which we have undertaken was all nothing. But it is not so, for we need to fall, and we need to see it; for if we did not fall, we should not know how feeble and how wretched we are in ourselves, nor, too, should we know so completely the wonderful love of our Creator.

For we shall truly see in heaven without end that we have sinned grievously in this life; and notwithstanding this, we shall truly see that we were never hurt in his love, nor were we ever of less value in his sight. And by the experience of this falling we shall have a great and marvellous knowledge of love in God without end; for enduring and marvellous is that love which cannot and will not be broken because of offences.

And this was one profitable understanding; another is the humility and meekness which we shall obtain by the sight of our fall, for by that we shall be raised high in heaven, to which raising we might never have come without that meekness. And therefore we need to see it; and if we do not see it, though we fell, that would not profit us. And commonly we first fall and then see it; and both are from the mercy of God.

The mother may sometimes suffer the child to fall and to be distressed in various ways, for its own benefit, but she can never suffer any kind of peril to come to her child, because of her love. And though our earthly mother may suffer her child to perish, our heavenly Mother Jesus may never suffer us who are his children to perish, for he is almighty, all wisdom and all love, and so is none but he, blessed may he be.

But often when our falling and our wretchedness are shown to us, we are so much afraid and so greatly ashamed of ourselves that we scarcely know where we can put ourselves. But then our courteous Mother does not wish us to flee away, for nothing would be less pleasing to him; but he then wants us to behave like a child. For when it is distressed and frightened, it runs quickly to its mother; and if it can do no more, it calls to the mother for help with all its might. So he wants us to act as a meek child, saying: My kind Mother, my gracious Mother, my beloved Mother, have mercy on me. I have made myself filthy and unlike you, and I may not and cannot make it right except with your help and grace.

And if we do not then feel ourselves eased, let us at once be sure that he is behaving as a wise Mother. For if he sees that it is profitable to us to mourn and to weep, with compassion and pity he suffers that until the right time has come, out of his love. And then he wants us to show a child's characteristics, which always naturally trusts in its mother's love in well-being and in woe. And he wants us to commit ourselves fervently to the faith of Holy Church, and find there our beloved Mother in consolation and true understanding, with all the company of the blessed. For one single person may often be broken, as it seems to him, but the entire body of Holy Church was never broken, nor ever will be without end. And therefore it is a certain thing, and good and gracious to will, meekly and fervently, to be fastened and united to our mother Holy Church, who is Christ Jesus. For the flood of mercy which is his dear blood and precious water is plentiful to make us fair and clean. The blessed wounds of our saviour are open and rejoice to heal us. The sweet gracious hands of our Mother are ready and diligent about us; for he in all this work exercises the true office of a kind nurse, who has nothing else to do but attend to the safety of her child.

It is his office to save us, it is his glory to do it, and it is his will that we know it; for he wants us to love him sweetly and trust in him meekly and greatly. And he revealed this in these gracious words: I protect you very safely.

THE SIXTY-SECOND CHAPTER

For at that time he revealed our frailty and our falling, our tres-
passes and our humiliations, our chagrins and our burdens and all our
woe, as much as it seemed to me could happen in this life. And with
that he revealed his blessed power, his blessed wisdom, his blessed
love, and that he protects us at such times, as tenderly and as sweetly, to
his glory, and as surely to our salvation as he does when we are in the
greatest consolation and comfort, and raises us to this in spirit, on
high in heaven, and turns everything to his glory and to our joy without end. For his precious love, he never allows us to lose time; and all
this is of the natural goodness of God by the operation of grace.

God is essence in his very nature; that is to say, that goodness
which is natural is God. He is the ground, his is the substance, he is
very essence or nature, and he is the true Father and the true Mother
of natures. And all natures which he has made to flow out of him to
work his will, they will be restored and brought back into him by the
salvation of man through the operation of grace. For all natures which
he has put separately in different creatures are all in man, wholly, in
fulness and power, in beauty and in goodness, in kingliness and in
nobility, in every manner of stateliness, preciousness and honour.

Here we can see that we are all bound to God by nature, and
we are bound to God by grace. Here we can see that we do not
need to seek far afield so as to know various natures, but to go to
Holy Church, into our Mother's breast, that is to say into our own
soul, where our Lord dwells. And there we should find everything,
now in faith and understanding, and afterwards truly, in himself,
clearly, in bliss.

But let no man or woman apply this particularly to himself,
because it is not so. It is general, because it is our precious Mother
Christ, and for him was this fair nature prepared for the honour
and the nobility of man's creation, and for the joy and the bliss of
man's salvation, just as he saw, knew and recognized from without
beginning.

THE SIXTY-THIRD CHAPTER

Here we may see that truly it belongs to our nature to hate sin, and truly it belongs to us by grace to hate sin, for nature is all good and fair in itself, and grace was sent out to save nature and destroy sin, and bring fair nature back again to the blessed place from which it came, which is God, with more nobility and honour by the powerful operation of grace. For it will be seen before God by all his saints in joy without end that nature has been tried in the fire of tribulation, and that no lack or defect is found in it.

So are nature and grace of one accord; for grace is God, as uncreated nature is God. He is two in his manner of operation, and one in love, and neither of these works without the other, and they are not separated. And when we by the mercy of God and with his help reconcile ourselves to nature and to grace, we shall see truly that sin is incomparably worse, more vile and painful than hell. For it is in opposition to our fair nature; for as truly as sin is unclean, so truly is sin unnatural. All this is a horrible thing to see for the loving soul which would wish to be all fair and shining in the sight of God, as nature and grace teach. But do not let us be afraid of this, except insofar as fear may be profitable; but let us meekly lament to our beloved Mother, and he will sprinkle us all with his precious blood, and make our soul most pliable and most mild, and heal us most gently in the course of time, just as it is most glory to him and joy to us without end. And from this sweet and gentle operation he will never cease or desist, until all his beloved children are born and brought to birth; and he revealed that when he gave understanding of the spiritual thirst which is the longing in love which will last till the day of judgment.

So in our true Mother Jesus our life is founded in his own prescient wisdom from without beginning, with the great power of the Father and the supreme goodness of the Holy Spirit. And in accepting our nature he gave us life, and in his blessed dying on the cross he bore us to endless life. And since that time, now and ever until the day of judgment, he feeds us and fosters us, just as the great supreme lovingness of motherhood wishes, and as the natural need of childhood asks. Fair and sweet is our heavenly Mother in the sight of our soul, precious and lovely are the children of grace in the sight of our heavenly Mother, with gentleness and meekness and all the lovely virtues which belong to children by nature. For the child does not naturally despair of the mother's love, the child does not naturally rely upon itself, naturally the child loves the mother and either of them the other.

These, and all others that resemble them, are such fair virtues, with which our heavenly Mother is served and pleased. And I understood no greater stature in this life than childhood, with its feebleness and lack of power and intelligence, until the time that our gracious Mother has brought us up into our Father's bliss. And there it will truly be made known to us what he means in the sweet words when he says: All will be well, and you will see it yourself, that every kind of thing will be well. And then will the bliss of our motherhood in Christ be to begin anew in the joys of our Father, God, which new beginning will last, newly beginning without end.

Chapter 4

SELF-IMPROVEMENT:

Gregory of Nyssa's Way of Perfection

How does one make one's self better, and what are the limits and goals of perfection? These are issues that confront us all in every walk of life.

Ultimately all questions about shaping the good life may be reduced to questions about the potentials of human nature. How good we think society can become is a function of how good we believe human nature is. Religion has always had a good deal to say about the potentials of human nature for good and evil. Traditionally these ideas are referred to as a doctrine of perfection.

Some religious groups known as "perfectionists" believe the spiritual life is all onward and upward, moving from glory to glory in anticipation of the great day of the Lord's return. Suffering, death, and failure all have a very limited part to play. They abide as irritants, marginal forces that will someday all be erased. The more in this life we believe, the more we move into that heavenly life in which there is no death. If we think right, in other words, those unpleasant things will go away.

Certainly this understanding of perfection is not at all limited to religious groups such as Pentecostals. In a secular version, it is very much part of the success ethic of contemporary American society. The good life means going from bigger to bigger houses and every year being treated to fatter paychecks, promotions, and honors. If we are not attaining those things, we are in a "dead-end" job, which implies that we are in a state of nonbeing. Life is success. Anything less is not life; we are not living up to our potential, not really living at all.

The way out of this state of nonbeing is to begin to think differently, to take charge of one's life, to believe in one's self. This is all very similar to the religious perfectionist believing in God's promises for the good life. The great difference, of course, is that the secular person who believes in himself may go out and take the appropriate actions that will often result in some betterment of the situation. The religious person, conversely, believes in God and often does little more, somehow thinking that unless it happens without one's efforts, it is not truly a divine occurrence. So, of course, most often nothing does happen, or at least nothing happens as anticipated. So the religious perfectionist may stay poor while a self-infatuated sybaritic secularist grows fat. In such situations, the believer becomes expert at looking beneath the surface of things to find meaning. "Oh, the secularist isn't really happy driving his new Jaguar." "He doesn't have any inner peace; that's why he has to wear such expensive clothes." The secularist, though, does not agree. She is very happy in that new Jag and Armani suit, so happy that she's off working toward another very tangible goal so she can buy more. The secularist's view of the perfect life fits nicely with her own experience. Perhaps she has modified her understanding slightly—success requires more hard work than she thought and it comes more slowly than she would like—but essentially all the pieces fit. The believer might not be so lucky. He is faced with a tremendous cognitive dissonance that screams in his ears whenever he cares to listen.

The way out of this dilemma for the person of faith is to readjust his or her understanding of self-improvement. If a "perfect" life means one that is without faults and foibles, or one in which our religious faith assures us material success, then one is left with unrealistic goals. Believing harder will not make one stop being an imperfect human being. Nor is it likely to make one rich. If, however, leading a perfect life means something else, something we are actually able to do, something for which we were made and which conforms to our natures, then we may progress, even in this life, toward the goal.

Gregory of Nyssa offered one such vision of the perfect life, one that can be as liberating for us as it was for those who first heard it in the fourth century.

WHO WAS GREGORY OF NYSSA?

Gregory of Nyssa was one of the Cappadocian Fathers of the Church, so named because of the town of Nyssa, which is in the region of Cappodocia in Asia Minor. He was born around 332 into one of the most extraordinary families of the early church. His parents, two brothers, and sister were all canonized as saints. His elder brother, Basil, persuaded Gregory to accept appointment as bishop of Nyssa in 372. So Gregory at age forty became a public spokesman for Christianity, something he had not done before. During the Council of Constantinople in 381 he devoted himself to the question of the Trinity and made important contributions in the fight against the heresy of Arianism, which denied the human nature of Jesus. Toward the end of his life he focused his attention on matters of the spiritual life.

Gregory is known as a philosophical theologian, because he built his understanding of God on the dominant Neoplatonism of his age. He lived at a time when Christianity was coming to grips with the culture of Hellenism. No longer a persecuted minority, Christians by the end of the fourth century were able to engage the mainstream of contemporary culture. An essential part of this process involved making a viable case for the truth of Christianity.

His debt to Greek philosophy is apparent in his writing. He accepts Aristotle's idea of virtue as the golden mean and throughout is constantly aware of the major outlines of Plato's thought. Indeed Gregory attempts to interpret Christian asceticism as a continuation of the contemplative life as spoken of by Plato.

HIS MESSAGE

Gregory's writing is filled with vivid images taken from the everyday experiences of life. A piece of wax, a rusted knife, a cliff overlooking the ocean all become icons through which he sees the spiritual world.

One of his most famous works is the *Life of Moses,* probably written in the 390s during Gregory's old age. Prepared for a friend who was a young seeker, the book is the old sage's advice on how to live a better life. The subject of the work is the perfect life, what it is and how to attain it. As was popular in those days, the work is a meditation on a biblical character, Moses. It begins with a brief preface, followed by a paraphrase of the story of the life of Moses as told in Exodus. What comes next is a section in which the spiritual meaning of the scriptural narrative is given. The book ends with a short conclusion summarizing what was said.

The preface opens with the story of a man at a horse race. Gregory tells how the man cheers for his horse to win, waving his hands about, motioning the rider on, shouting encouragement and advice. Gregory is like that fan, and the quest for perfection is like the race. His book is an effort to help those who read it run the race of life with success.

Despite his good intentions, Gregory complains that giving an outline of the perfect life is too demanding a task; the boundaries of perfection are such that they elude both his attempts to speak of them and his efforts to live them. Nevertheless, there are some things about the perfect life that he does know and can share.

The first among these is that the quest for a perfect life is dynamic. We are always either moving forward toward virtue or back toward evil. To grow in goodness is the object of perfection. The more one attains what is good, the more one wants of the good.

Is there ever a point at which one has enough of what is good? To understand Gregory's answer, we must know that for him goodness can only be described in reference to the one who is Goodness itself. In Gregory's words: "…whoever pursues true virtue participates in nothing other than God, because He is Himself absolute virtue" [I.7]. Because God is Himself limitless, participation in God is a limitless, endless process. Every act by which we grow in virtue causes us to share in more and more of the divine nature. The perfection of human nature consists, then, in its very growth in goodness.

All of this becomes clear from the spiritual meaning of the story of Moses. Moses' life is a journey from the land of his birth, through the desert to the holy mountain of Sinai on which he meets with God and goes on to lead his people to the promised land. For Gregory the story of Moses is more than an account of the founding of the nation of Israel. It is an allegory for the journey of life. Whether the story is an accurate historical account of the wanderings of the tribes of Israel during the Exodus does not concern him. He certainly does not care about the historical circumstances in which the book of Exodus was written. He instinctively realizes that at its most profound level the biblical story is about the soul and, as such, has a mystical significance to all of us who have souls.

We all must travel from the bondage of Egypt to the freedom of the promised land. We are all challenged to follow the Spirit into a life of greater and greater participation in the divine. And along that journey we are all confronted, often in the most perplexing manner, with revelations of the transcendent.

For Moses there were two great theophanies that marked his life: the burning bush in the desert and the cloud on Mount Sinai.

When Moses saw the burning bush he had an apprehension of the true nature of Being. At that moment when he gazed upon the bush that burned but was not consumed by the flames he realized that the transcendent essence and cause of the universe on which everything depends, which alone subsists, which is always the same, immutable to all change, standing in need of nothing, alone desirable, participated in by all but not lessened is real Being.

That moment of enlightenment is the moment in which we understand the difference between truth and falsehood in its most profound degree. We see the gap between the illusory and the permanent, between things of passing value and the eternal.

The next theophany in Moses' life occurred on Mount Sinai when he ascended the mountain to obtain the ten commandments from the Lord. As he climbed higher Moses went deeper and deeper into a cloud. It was in the darkness of the cloud, where his eyes could hardly see, that he had the most profound encounter with the living God. The journey that began with the illumination of the burning bush led to an encounter with God in darkness.

The lesson of the allegory is, in Gregory's words:

> As the mind progresses it gains access to the invisible and the incomprehensible and there it sees God. This is the true knowledge of what is sought; this is the seeing that consists of not seeing, because that which is sought transcends all knowledge, being separated on all sides by incomprehensibility as by a kind of darkness. [II.163]

If nothing hinders the soul's ascent it moves through the limitations of its own physical senses to a higher plain of consciousness in which it perceives what is good, true, and beautiful as it partakes in its Divine Source. Progress in perfection, then, is eternal. The soul longs for God. The seeker of perfection is an ardent, passionate lover of the Divine Beauty. He receives what is visible as but an image of what he desires—and longs to be filled with the very stamp of the Archetype.

Yet there is something that can and does hinder the process. Whenever one chooses to love something other than the Divine Source, one moves away from that source and becomes mired in the shadows, confused and lost, seeking what is imperfect and changing, rather than the immutable and eternal. Human nature is endowed with a desire for goodness that can only be satisfied in God, but that desire can be muted and perverted in its quest by the lusts of the flesh and the cares of the material world.

There is always a struggle between good and evil, but it is not a struggle that the seeker need ultimately lose. This is because we have been created in the image of God. That image is like a piece of precious, lustrous metal. It has become tarnished by rust so that its brilliance is dulled. Such is the result of sin. But if we wash off, by the practice of virtue, the filth that has stuck on that image like a corrosive film, the Divine Beauty again will shine forth.

Another way Gregory presents this is by comparing the process to a man looking at the sun in a mirror. He is not able to gaze at the sun directly, for he is too weak. Yet in the reflection, in the image of the sun on the glass, he sees the strength and force of the sun. Gregory tenderly and confidently continues: "Even though you are too weak to perceive the Light Itself, yet, if you but return to the grace of the Image with which you were informed from the beginning, you will have all you seek in yourselves."

Here is a moving statement of the notion of image mysticism that has one of its earliest voices in Gregory. The tradition is taken up by Gregory's contemporary Augustine and later by the sixth-century writer, the Pseudo-Dionysius. From those seminals it spreads throughout both Western and Eastern Christian thought, providing the basis for, among other things, the Christian humanism of the Renaissance, theories on the relation of religion and aesthetics, such as those offered by Urs von Balthasar in our own time, and the rich understanding of sanctification as divinization found in Byzantine Christianity.

How do we cleanse our souls of the stain that keeps divine beauty from shining forth? By obeying God and living and thinking in a way that focuses us on the grace of the Image. God's instructions on how to live the good life are like a plow that digs up the evil roots from the depths of our hearts. They remove evil not only from our actions, but from inner thoughts as well. We then must "lay aside the evil mask and put on again the Divine Image."

The way of perfection obviously requires discipline. It involves choosing good over evil, denying our base tendencies, and loving what is best, purest, and most excellent.

The process of perfection is never ending. It does not mean "success" as we think of it, either in material terms as more money and junk, or in churchly terms as bigger congregations, or in personal terms as coming to the point where we no longer have any questions or problems. Rather it is essentially growing in the mystery of God, walking deeper into the cloud, learning how to live with uncertainty, realizing that we are on a never-ending pilgrimage. That is an idea that has real importance for everyday life. Perfection is not living without imperfections. It is living in God, choosing each moment to love what is ultimately good, true, and beautiful, striving to live virtuously, and occasionally being dazzled by the divine as we are surprised by its epiphanies.

The seeing that consists in not seeing. That is the paradox, the challenge, the joy of Gregory's great insight about how to live the good life. It cannot be trivialized. One cannot simply list the steps to learn it. It stands in all its force, all its offense, all its wonder.

BIBLIOGRAPHY

From Glory to Glory: Texts from Gregory of Nyssa's Mystical Writings. Trans. Herbert Musurillo. New York: Charles Scribner's Sons, 1961.

Gregory of Nyssa: The Life of Moses. Trans. Abraham J. Malherbe and Everett Ferguson. The Classics of Western Spirituality. New York/Ramsey, N.J.: Paulist Press, 1978.

The Lord's Prayer; The Beatitudes, trans. Hilda Graef. Westminster, Md.: Newman Press, 1954.

LIFE OF MOSES[5]

PROLOGUE

1. At horse races the spectators intent on victory shout to their favorites in the contest, even though the horses are eager to run. From the stands they participate in the race with their eyes, thinking to incite the charioteer to keener effort, at the same time urging the horses on while leaning forward and flailing the air with their outstretched hands instead of with a whip. They do this not because their actions themselves contribute anything to the victory; but in this way, by their good will, they eagerly show in voice and deed their concern for the contestants. I seem to be doing the same thing myself, most valued friend and brother. While you are competing admirably in the divine race along the course of virtue, lightfootedly leaping and straining constantly for the *prize of the heavenly calling,* I exhort, urge and encourage you vigorously to increase your speed. I do this, not moved to it by some unconsidered impulse, but to humor the delights of a beloved child.

2. Since the letter which you recently sent requested us to furnish you with some counsel concerning the perfect life, I thought it only proper to answer your request. Although there may be nothing useful for you in my words, perhaps this example of ready obedience will not be wholly unprofitable to you. For if we who have been appointed to the position of fathers over so many souls consider it proper here in our old age to accept a commission from youth, how much more suitable is it, inasmuch as we

---

5. *Gregory of Nyssa: The Life of Moses,* trans. Abraham J. Malherbe and Everett Ferguson, the Classics of Western Spirituality (New York/Ramsey, N.J.: Paulist Press, 1978).

have taught you, a young man, to obey voluntarily, that the right action of ready obedience be confirmed in you.

3. So much for that. We must take up the task that lies before us, taking God as our guide in our treatise. You requested, dear friend, that we trace in outline for you what the perfect life is. Your intention clearly was to translate the grace disclosed by my word into your own life, if you should find in my treatise what you were seeking. I am at an equal loss about both things: It is beyond my power to encompass perfection in my treatise or to show in my life the insights of the treatise. And perhaps I am not alone in this. Many great men, even those who excel in virtue, will admit that for them such an accomplishment as this is unattainable.

4. As I would not seem, in the words of the Psalmist, *there to tremble for fear, where no fear was,* I shall set forth for you more clearly what I think.

5. The perfection of everything which can be measured by the senses is marked off by certain definite boundaries. Quantity, for example, admits of both continuity and limitation, for every quantitative measure is circumscribed by certain limits proper to itself. The person who looks at a cubit or at the number ten knows that its perfection consists in the fact that it has both a beginning and an end. But in the case of virtue we have learned from the Apostle that its one limit of perfection is the fact that it has no limit. For that divine Apostle, great and lofty in understanding, ever running the course of virtue, never ceased *straining toward those things that are still to come.* Coming to a stop in the race was not safe for him. Why? Because no Good has a limit in its own nature but is limited by the presence of its opposite, as life is limited by death and light by darkness. And every good thing generally ends with all those things which are perceived to be contrary to the good.

6. Just as the end of life is the beginning of death, so also stopping in the race of virtue marks the beginning of the race of evil. Thus our statement that grasping perfection with reference to virtue is impossible was not false, for it has been pointed out that what is marked off by boundaries is not virtue.

I said that it is also impossible for those who pursue the life of virtue to attain perfection. The meaning of this statement will be explained.

7. The Divine One is himself the Good (in the primary and proper sense of the word), whose very nature is goodness. This he is and he is so named, and is known by this nature. Since, then, it has not been demonstrated that there is any limit to virtue except evil, and since the Divine does not admit of an opposite, we hold the divine nature to be unlimited and infinite. Certainly whoever pursues true virtue participates in nothing other than God, because he is himself absolute virtue. Since, then, those who know what is good by nature desire participation in it, and since this good has no limit, the participant's desire itself necessarily has no stopping place but stretches out with the limitless.

8. It is therefore undoubtedly impossible to attain perfection, since, as I have said, perfection is not marked off by limits: The one limit of virtue is the absence of a limit. How then would one arrive at the sought-for boundary when he can find no boundary?

9. Although on the whole my argument has shown that what is sought for is unattainable, one should not disregard the commandment of the Lord which says, *Therefore be perfect, just as your heavenly father is perfect.* For in the case of those things which are good by nature, even if men of understanding were not able to attain to everything, by attaining even a part they could yet gain a great deal.

10. We should show great diligence not to fall away from the perfection which is attainable but to acquire as much as is possible: To that extent let us make progress within the realm of what we seek. For the perfection of human nature consists perhaps in its very growth in goodness.

11. It seems good to me to make use of Scripture as a counselor in this matter. For the divine voice says somewhere in the prophecy of Isaiah, *Consider Abraham your father, and Sarah who gave you birth.* Scripture gives this admonition to those who wander outside virtue. Just as at sea those who are carried away from the

direction of the harbor bring themselves back on course by a clear sign, upon seeing either a beacon light raised up high or some mountain peak coming into view, in the same way Scripture by the example of Abraham and Sarah may guide again to the harbor of the divine will those adrift on the sea of life with a pilotless mind.

12. Human nature is divided into male and female, and the free choice of virtue or of evil is set before both equally. For this reason the corresponding example of virtue for each sex has been exemplified by the divine voice, so that each, by observing the one to which he is akin (the men to Abraham and the women to Sarah), may be directed in the life of virtue by the appropriate examples.

13. Perhaps, then, the memory of anyone distinguished in life would be enough to fill our need for a beacon light and to show us how we can bring our soul to the sheltered harbor of virtue where it no longer has to pass the winter amid the storms of life or be shipwrecked in the deep water of evil by the successive billows of passion. It may be for this very reason that the daily life of those sublime individuals is recorded in detail, that by imitating those earlier examples of right action those who follow them may conduct their lives to the good.

14. What then? Some one will say, "How shall I imitate them, since I am not a Chaldaean as I remember Abraham was, nor was I nourished by the daughter of the Egyptian as Scripture teaches about Moses, and in general I do not have in these matters anything in my life corresponding to anyone of the ancients? How shall I place myself in the same rank with one of them, when I do not know how to imitate anyone so far removed from me by the circumstances of his life?" To him we reply that we do not consider being a Chaldaean a virtue or a vice, nor is anyone exiled from the life of virtue by living in Egypt or spending his life in Babylon, nor again has God been known to the esteemed individuals in Judaea only, nor is Zion, as people commonly think, the divine habitation. We need some subtlety of understanding and keenness of vision to discern from the history how, by removing ourselves from such

Chaldaeans and Egyptians and by escaping from such a Babylonian captivity, we shall embark on the blessed life.

15. Let us put forth Moses as our example for life in our treatise. First we shall go through in outline his life as we have learned it from the divine Scriptures. Then we shall seek out the spiritual understanding which corresponds to the history in order to obtain suggestions of virtue. Through such understanding we may come to know the perfect life for men.

★   ★   ★

ETERNAL PROGRESS

219. While following these things in the sequence of our investigation, we were led to a deeper meaning in contemplating this passage. Let us return to the subject. How does someone who Scripture says saw God clearly in such divine appearances—*face to face, as a man speaks with his friend*—require that God appear to him, as though he who is always visible had not yet been seen, as though Moses had not yet attained what Scripture testifies he had indeed attained?

220. The heavenly voice now grants the petitioner's request and does not deny this additional grace. Yet again He leads him to despair in that He affirms that what the petitioner seeks cannot be contained by human life. Still, God says there is a *place with himself* where there is a *rock with a hole in it* into which he commands Moses to enter. Then God placed his hand over the mouth of the hole and called out to Moses as he passed by. When Moses was summoned, he came out of the hole and saw the back of the One who called him. In this way he thought he saw what he was seeking, and the promise of the divine voice did not prove false.

221. If these things are looked at literally, not only will the understanding of those who seek God be dim, but their concept of him will also be inappropriate. Front and back pertain only to those things which are observed to have shape. Every shape provides the limits of a body. So then he who conceives of God in some shape

will not realize that he is free of a bodily nature. It is a fact that every body is composite, that what is composite exists by the joining of its different elements. No one would say that what is composite cannot be decomposed. And what decomposes cannot be incorruptible, for corruption is the decomposition of what is composite.

222. If therefore one should think of the back of God in a literal fashion, he will necessarily be carried to such an absurd conclusion. For front and back pertain to a shape, and shape pertains to a body. A body by its very nature can be decomposed, for everything composite is capable of dissolution. But what is being decomposed cannot be incorruptible; therefore, he who is bound to the letter would consequently conceive the Divine to be corruptible. But in fact God is incorruptible and incorporeal.

223. But what understanding other than the literal interpretation fits what is written? If this part of the written narrative compels us to seek out another understanding, it is certainly appropriate to understand the whole in the same way. Whatever we perceive in the part, we of necessity take as true for the whole, since every whole is made up of its parts. Wherefore the place with God, the rock at that place, the opening in it called a hole, Moses' entrance into it, the placing of the divine hand over its mouth, the passing by and the calling and after this the vision of the back—all this would more fittingly be contemplated in its spiritual sense.

224. What then is being signified? Bodies, once they have received the initial thrust downward, are driven downward by themselves with greater speed without any additional help as long as the surface on which they move is steadily sloping and no resistance to their downward thrust is encountered. Similarly, the soul moves in the opposite direction. Once it is released from its earthly attachment, it becomes light and swift for its movement upward, soaring from below up to the heights.

225. If nothing comes from above to hinder its upward thrust (for the nature of the Good attracts to itself those who look to it), the soul rises ever higher and will always make its flight yet

higher—by its desire of the heavenly things *straining ahead for what is still to come,* as the Apostle says.

226. Made to desire and not to abandon the transcendent height by the things already attained, it makes its way upward without ceasing, ever through its prior accomplishments renewing its intensity for the flight. Activity directed toward virtue causes its capacity to grow through exertion; this kind of activity alone does not slacken its intensity by the effort, but increases it.

227. For this reason we also say that the great Moses, as he was becoming ever greater, at no time stopped in his ascent, nor did he set a limit for himself in his upward course. Once having set foot on the ladder which God set up (as Jacob says), he continually climbed to the step above and never ceased to rise higher, because he always found a step higher than the one he had attained.

228. He denied the specious kinship with the Egyptian queen. He avenged the Hebrew. He chose the desert way of life where there was no human being to disturb him. In himself he shepherded a flock of tame animals. He saw the brilliance of the light. Unencumbered, having taken off his sandals, he made his approach to the light. He brought his kinsmen and countrymen out to freedom. He saw the enemy drowning in the sea.

229. He made camps under the cloud. He quenched thirst with the rock. He produced bread from heaven. By stretching out his hands, he overcame the foreigner. He heard the trumpet. He entered the darkness. He slipped into the inner sanctuary of the tabernacle not made with hands. He learned the secrets of the divine priesthood. He destroyed the idol. He supplicated the divine Being. He restored the Law destroyed by the evil of the Jews.

230. He shone with glory. And although lifted up through such lofty experiences, he is still unsatisfied in his desire for more. He still thirsts for that with which he constantly filled himself to capacity, and he asks to attain as if he had never partaken, beseeching God to appear to him, not according to his capacity to partake, but according to God's true being.

231. Such an experience seems to me to belong to the soul which loves what is beautiful. Hope always draws the soul from the beauty which is seen to what is beyond, always kindles the desire for the hidden through what is constantly perceived. Therefore, the ardent love of beauty, although receiving what is always visible as an image of what he desires, yet longs to be filled with the very stamp of the archetype.

232. And the bold request which goes up the mountains of desire asks this: to enjoy the Beauty not in mirrors and reflections, but face to face. The divine voice granted what was requested in what was denied, showing in a few words an immeasurable depth of thought. The munificence of God assented to the fulfillment of his desire, but did not promise any cessation or satiety of the desire.

233. He would not have shown himself to his servant if the sight were such as to bring the desire of the beholder to an end, since the true sight of God consists in this, that the one who looks up to God never ceases in that desire. For he says: *You cannot see my face, for man cannot see me and live.*

234. Scripture does not indicate that this causes the death of those who look, for how would the face of life ever be the cause of death to those who approach it? On the contrary, the Divine is by its nature life-giving. Yet the characteristic of the divine nature is to transcend all characteristics. Therefore, he who thinks God is something to be known does not have life, because he has turned from true Being to what he considers by sense perception to have being.

235. True Being is true life. This Being is inaccessible to knowledge. If then the life-giving nature transcends knowledge, that which is perceived certainly is not life. It is not in the nature of what is not life to be the cause of life. Thus, what Moses yearned for is satisfied by the very things which leave his desire unsatisfied.

236. He learns from what was said that the Divine is by its very nature infinite, enclosed in no boundary. If the Divine is perceived as though bounded by something, one must by all means consider along with that boundary what is beyond it. For certainly that which is bounded leaves off at some point, as air provides the

boundary for all that flies and water for all that live in it. Therefore, fish are surrounded on every side by water, and birds by air. The limits of the boundaries which circumscribe the birds or the fish are obvious: The water is the limit to what swims and the air to what flies. In the same way, God, if he is conceived as bounded, would necessarily be surrounded by something different in nature. It is only logical that what encompasses is much larger than what is contained.

237. Now it is agreed that the Divine is good in nature. But what is different in nature from the Good is surely something other than the Good. What is outside the Good is perceived to be evil in nature. But it was shown that what encompasses is much larger than what is encompassed. It most certainly follows, then, that those who think God is bounded conclude that he is enclosed by evil.

238. Since what is encompassed is certainly less than what encompasses, it would follow that the stronger prevails. Therefore, he who enclosed the Divine by any boundary makes out that the Good is ruled over by its opposite. But that is out of the question. Therefore, no consideration will be given to anything enclosing infinite nature. It is not in the nature of what is unenclosed to be grasped. But every desire for the Good which is attracted to that ascent constantly expands as one progresses in pressing on to the Good.

239. This truly is the vision of God: never to be satisfied in the desire to see him. But one must always, by looking at what he can see, rekindle this desire to see more. Thus, no limit would interrupt growth in the ascent to God, since no limit to the Good can be found nor is the increasing of desire for the Good brought to an end because it is satisfied.

240. But what is that place which is seen next to God? What is the rock? And what again is the hole in the rock? What is the hand of God that covers the mouth of the rock? What is the passing by of God? What is his back which God promised to Moses when he asked to see him face to face?

241. Naturally each of these things must be highly significant and worthy of the munificence of the divine Giver. Thus this promise is believed to be more magnificent and loftier than every

theophany which had previously been granted to his great servant. How then would one, from what has been said, understand this height to which Moses desires to attain after such previous ascents and to which *he who turns everything to their good cooperates with all those who love God* makes the ascent easy through his leadership? *Here is a place,* he says, *beside me.*

242. The thought harmonizes readily with what has been contemplated before. In speaking of "place" he does not limit *the place* indicated by anything quantitative (for to something unquantitative there is no measure). On the contrary, by the use of the analogy of a measurable surface he leads the hearer to the unlimited and infinite. The text seems to signify some such understanding: "Whereas, Moses, your desire for *what is still to come* has expanded and you have not reached satisfaction in your progress and whereas you do not see any limit to the Good, but your yearning always looks for more, the place with me is so great that the one running in it is never able to cease from his progress."

243. In another Scriptural passage the progress is a standing still, for it says, *You must stand on the rock.* This is the most marvelous thing of all: how the same thing is both a standing still and a moving. For he who ascends certainly does not stand still, and he who stands still does not move upwards. But here the ascent takes place by means of the standing. I mean by this that the firmer and more immovable one remains in the Good, the more he progresses in the course of virtue. The man who in his reasonings is uncertain and liable to slip, since he has no firm grounding in the Good but *is tossed one way and another and carried along* (as the Apostle says) and is doubtful and wavers in his opinions concerning reality, would never attain to the height of virtue.

244. He is like those who toil endlessly as they climb uphill in sand: Even though they take long steps, their footing in the sand always slips downhill, so that, although there is much motion, no progress results from it. But if someone, as the Psalmist says, should pull his feet up from the mud of the pit and plant them upon the rock (the rock is Christ who is absolute virtue), then the more

steadfast and unmoveable (according to the advice of Paul) he becomes in the Good the faster he completes the course. It is like using the standing still as if it were a wing while the heart flies upward through its stability in the good.

245. Therefore, he who showed Moses the place urges him on his course. When he promised that he would stand him on the rock, he showed him the nature of that divine race. But the opening in the rock which Scripture calls a "hole" the divine Apostle interprets well in his own words when he speaks of a heavenly house not made with hands which is laid up by hope for those who have dissolved their earthly tabernacle.

246. For truly he who has *run the race,* as the Apostle says, in that wide and roomy stadium, which the divine voice calls "place," and has *kept the faith* and, as the figurative expression says, has planted his feet on the rock; such a person will be adorned with the *crown of righteousness* from the hand of the contest's judge. This prize is described in different ways by Scripture.

247. For the same thing which is here called an opening in the rock is elsewhere referred to as "pleasure of paradise," "eternal tabernacle," "mansion with the Father," "bosom of the patriarch," "land of the living," "water of refreshment," "Jerusalem which is above," "kingdom of heaven," "prize of calling," "crown of graces," "crown of pleasure," "crown of beauty," "pillar of strength," "pleasure on a table," "councils of God," "throne of judgment," "place of name," "hidden tabernacle."

248. We say, then, that Moses' entrance into the rock has the same significance as these descriptions. For, since Christ is understood by Paul as the rock, all hope of good things is believed to be in Christ, in whom we have learned all the treasures of good things to be. He who finds any good finds it in Christ who contains all good.

249. He who attained to this and was shadowed by the hand of God, as the text promised (for the hand of God would be the creative power of what exists, the *only begotten God,* by whom *all things were made,* who is also "place" for those who run, who is,

according to his own words, the "way" of the course, and who is "rock" to those who are well established and "house" to those who are resting), he it is who will hear the One who summons and will see the back of the One who calls, which means he will *follow Yahweh your God,* as the Law commands.

250. When the great David heard and understood this, he said to him *who dwells in the shelter of the most High; He will overshadow you with his shoulders,* which is the same as being behind God (for the shoulder is on the back of the body). Concerning himself David says, *My soul clings close to you, your right hand supports me.* You see how the Psalms agree with the history. For as the one says that the right hand is a help to the person who has joined himself close behind God, so the other says that the hand touches the person who waits in the rock upon the divine voice and prays that he might follow behind.

251. But when the Lord who spoke to Moses came to fulfill his own law, he likewise gave a clear explanation to his disciples, laying bare the meaning of what had previously been said in a figure when he said, *If anyone wants to be a follower of mine* and not "If any man will go before me." And to the one asking about eternal life he proposes the same thing, for he says *Come, follow me.* Now, he who follows sees the back.

252. So Moses, who eagerly seeks to behold God, is now taught how he can behold Him: to follow God wherever he might lead is to behold God. His passing by signifies his guiding the one who follows, for someone who does not know the way cannot complete his journey safely in any other way than by following behind his guide. He who leads, then, by his guidance shows the way to the one following. He who follows will not turn aside from the right way if he always keeps the back of his leader in view.

253. For he who moves to one side or brings himself to face his guide assumes another direction for himself than the one his guide shows him. Therefore, he says to the one who is led, *My face is not to be seen,* that is "Do not face your guide." If he does so, his

course will certainly be in the opposite direction, for good does not look good in the face, but follows it.

254. What is perceived to be its opposite is face to face with the good, for what looks virtue in the face is evil. But virtue is not perceived in contrast to virtue. Therefore, Moses does not look God in the face, but looks at his back; for whoever looks at him face to face shall not live, as the divine voice testifies, *man cannot see* the face of the Lord *and live.*

255. You see how it is so great a thing to learn how to follow God, that after those lofty ascents and awesome and glorious theophanies virtually at the end of his life, the man who has learned to follow behind God is scarcely considered worthy of this grace.

Chapter 5

RELATING LOVE, EROS, AND GOD:

DANTE ALIGHIERI

Dante was born in Florence in 1265 and died an exile in Ravena in 1321. His masterwork, *The Divine Comedy,* was hailed in its own day as groundbreaking and went on to play an important role in the creation of modern Italian. Although he was not a trained theologian, his ideas have influenced Western spirituality. Most notably his ideas shaped St. Catherine of Genoa's idea of purgatory and were reflected in succeeding generations by authors as diverse as John Bunyan and T. S. Eliot.

Dante was the great poet of love, who told of the whole range of love and would not separate it into compartments, one divine, another earthly. Rather he fused our manifold loves into one.

Love. We hear it sung about virtually every time we turn on the radio. We hear it spoken about on all the talk shows. We tell our family we love them twice every day.

Eros. We are bathed in it, drowning in it, suffused with it, inundated by it. It is used to sell shampoo. To advertise beer. To sell underwear, movie tickets, even diet milk shakes. Pornography has been redefined. Once it was an unspeakable dirty secret enjoyed by odd little men sneaking into the back room of smoke shops to buy magazines. Once it was limited to the stag film, viewed the night before one's wedding with your buddies, a cigar, and a beer. It now has gone uptown. It's prime time. It's brought into our homes by cables and satellites. Beautiful young people flock to it as a way into Hollywood. Women watch it by themselves. Wives watch it with their husbands. College students consume it like soda. And the Internet pours an open pipe of the most sordid sort onto our desktops, our workplaces, our imaginations.

God. For many, if "God" means anything God means morality, and morality based on religion often means all of the sensuality and eroticism of today's culture is wrong and threatens to damage our souls.

Yet we are quite willing to relate God and love. We hear sermon after sermon on how much God loves us, on how much we should love one another, and how God and love are intimately related.

We also have no problem relating love and *eros*. It seems quite normal to do so, and the sexual revolution has made us more comfortable with it.

Relating God, love, and *eros* can be done, however. It requires, of course, a more nuanced view of *eros*, one that distinguishes *eros* from *pornos*, to be sure. Doing so is important, because otherwise the whole range of human love cannot be related to God, and all our talk about God and love is somehow incomplete. We are left to construct our own sexual morality, because we have never heard anything much other than what we should not do. Or we are left, in the case of Catholicism, for example, wondering how a religious tradition that makes asceticism, and most often, celibacy, a virtual imperative for the holy life can tell us how we should love our spouses.

Some will see little need to relate these three. They do not see the world in terms of God. But even they feel the fragmented nature of our loves. Even they have known the heartache that ensues when *eros* operates without charity. They have felt the emptiness of a cold, polite kindness where there is no passion. And they have participated in the absurdity of holding onto another human being even as the cruel universe pulled him away forever through its never-ending powers of decay. Without God, the religious voices claim, those tragedies have no hope of resolution. They are final and certain and they bring little hope in their wake.

Religion then has tried to speak of all three—God, love, and *eros*. Certainly other religions have done more than Christianity to discuss the relation among God, love, and sensuality. Hinduism has a rich tradition, as illustrated in the stories of the god Krishna seducing the gopi girls. Judaism also, in the Kabbalah traditions and the meditations about Shekhinah—the divine presence, the tenth *serirah*, the female partner of *Tif'eret*—offer fertile ideas.

In Christianity we have examples of this attempted relation, as well, even though they are often not well known. Bernard of Clairvaux, the twelfth-century Cistercian abbot, composed one of his most important works of theology in the form of a meditation on the great love poem of the Bible, the Song of Songs. Bernard characterized the highest union of God and the soul not in formal scholastic terms but as a kiss.

In addition to Bernard, there is Dante, more poet than theologian to be sure, yet serious in his God talk and not ignorant of the larger love tradition in Christian spirituality. Dante chooses Bernard, for example, as his final guide in the *Paradiso,* after Virgil and Beatrice can take him no further toward the beatific vision. In Dante there is much that can aid us on our own quest today to redeem and unite what our world has broken apart. Perhaps because he was a layperson, not a monk, he could address these issues more broadly in a language that can speak to us today.

DANTE'S *DIVINE COMEDY*

T. S. Eliot put it plainly: "Dante and Shakespeare divide the modern world between them; there is no third." Eliot looked to the great Florentine poet again and again for inspiration, quoting him repeatedly in his masterpiece, *The Waste Land* and other works. Nevertheless, Dante's presence in the modern world was limited to his literary patrimony. He lived three hundred years before Shakespeare, at the height of the Middle Ages. His poetry, suffused with the worldview of his times, is replete with the learning of the greatest theologians and philosophers of the age. If he is to be considered modern at all, it must only be in his ability to speak to us today.

Dante speaks to the heart of our age because he talks about love. Love is what we yearn for. Beneath our materialism and our hedonism, beneath our eroticism and our profligacy, we want to be loved. We want to be loved because like all human beings of every time we were made for love. But living in an industrialized world where the bonds of community have been broken under the hammer of the machine, we especially need to know we are different from our mechanical masters and capable of loving and of being loved.

Dante writes about the whole range of love. Excessive love distorted into lust, anger, and greed. Deficient love that breeds sloth. Misdirected love that drives envy, wrath, and pride. The love of God for human beings. The love of people for the highest good. The love of a man for a woman. The love of the angels for their maker. All is here on a cosmic plane reaching from the depths of hell to outer space. He creates a world, fantastic and wondrous, peopled not only with strange creatures but with real individuals who were part of his life in Florence.

When Dante was in what we would call a midlife crisis he began the creation of his masterpiece of poetry. It was when love had seemingly deserted him, when those whom he thought his friends betrayed him, that he found his way back to the love that heals and reunites us with our highest natures.

DANTE'S LIFE AND TIMES

On the banks of the Arno in Tuscany sits a city that is known the world over for its beauty. From Piazza San Michelangelo one can look down and see the red-tiled roofs shining against the tan-colored stone of the buildings. One can see the Ponte Vecchio, the Duomo, the Church of Sante Croce, and the Pitti Palace. One can see the grandeur, the beauty of the past and appreciate the wisdom of the Medici, the talent of Massacio, the genius of Michelangelo. It is all there to behold in a world-famous skyline.

But not so easily seen is the violence of the past that made Florence a city often drenched in the blood of its own, slain by its own. The only hint remaining in the city's architecture is the many towers. At first glance the modern eye accustomed to high-rise buildings in cities thinks nothing of them. But closer examination reveals that they were not the Trump Towers of their day. They were fortresses with few apertures and little beauty. They were built as shelters to protect people from their fellow citizens.

The Florence of Dante's day was not a city within a larger country so much as it was a city-state with its own claims to sovereignty and considerable influence on the Italian peninsula and throughout the region once controlled by the Roman Empire. Like other cities of northern Italy, it is aptly compared to the Greek city-states of antiquity, where individuals identified with the town. Membership in the *commune* was of the greatest importance for a Florentine. Apart from community, a person was lost, cast out from his particular place in the larger civilized order. For that reason forced exile from the city was viewed as a deathlike fate.

At the time of Dante's birth, Florence was entering a period of greatness and international renown. It was known throughout the world once dominated by the Roman Empire for its manufactured goods—wool, silks, furs, leather, and armaments—and its banks. Its commercial families trained their sons in the skills of international business. It was customary for at least one son to be sent off during his young manhood to a foreign city to learn the customs and language in order to develop opportunities for his family business. Florence was undoubtedly one of the wealthiest cities of the late Middle Ages in Europe.

Some of that wealth was gotten by what was considered at the time illicit means. Florentine banks lent money to businesses throughout Europe. The city's currency, the florin, was the most widely accepted of its time. There modern banking found its beginnings; but all in violation of a basic law of the church, dating back to origin of Christian communities, that forbade the lending of money at interest. Because the civil law of the day was closely tied to church law, no laws regulated usury; it was simply forbidden, even though everyone winked at the prohibition. The banks carried on outside the law and were never seriously punished for it. In fact, the papacy itself by Dante's time had become dependent on the banks in some measure for its own finances.

Unlike the earlier feudal towns of the Middle Ages, Florence was a city of commerce, a town of the bourgeoisie. Both the former feudal lords and the traders, bankers, and craftsmen engaged in business and made money not primarily from the land or from their patrimonies but from a nascent form of capitalism that prospered in this democratic city-state.

The absence of a king made the rivalry among Florentines for political power all the more open and spirited. For much of the period immediately following Dante's birth, the rivalry for power centered on two groups, the Ghibellines and the Guelfs. The Ghibellines were the scions of the feudal lords. They looked to the north of Italy for support, to the princes of Germany and France, and to the Holy Roman Emperor. The Guelfs had their origin among the guilds of craftsmen and the bankers. Their allegiance was to the pope, who, as a temporal power, was eager to support any group that would limit the prerogatives of kings, who had been locked in a power struggle with the popes since the time of Charlemagne.

The Guelfs had decisively defeated the Ghibellines in the battle of Benvento and were firmly in control of Florence in 1266, one year after Dante's birth. Dante's family was a typical merchant-class family, loyal to the Guelfs. But the memberships of and allegiances to the traditional parties were changing especially after the defeat of the Ghibellines and their feudal sympathizers. There arose in its place a division between two wings of the Guelfs called the Whites and the Blacks.

The Whites, the party to which Dante belonged, consisted mainly of the merchants, whose wealth was relatively new. The Blacks represented families like the Donati, who owned the Florentine banks. Their interest was in expanding the international influence of the city so as to broaden their own financial business. The Blacks had the backing of a papacy that needed to curry the good graces of the bankers. The rivalry between the two groups erupted into bloodshed in 1300. Bonafazio VIII intervened and sided with the Blacks, sending a papal legate to Florence ostensibly to make peace. Instead the legate opened the city to the armed forces of a Black, Corso di Donati, who ousted the White leaders and either killed or imprisoned them.

Dante, until 1300, had been focused on a career in public service and, to a much lesser extent, on the growth of his skills as a poet. The public Dante served in the city government. At the peak of his career at age thirty-seven, he attained a post on the ruling counsel of Florence called the Signoria. With the Black victory in 1300, Dante, who was fortunately outside of the city at the time of the Blacks' takeover, was exiled for life. A return to the city would have meant death or prison, so for the final nineteen years of his life he lived in the homes of friends and patrons in Verona, in Sarzana, and other northern Italian cities.

Far more important than his activities as a civil servant were his efforts as a poet. His writing career began with the *Vita Nuova,* a collection of poems he wrote about his first love, Beatrice. Dante had met Beatrice when he was a boy in Florence. One cannot account for the exuberant, overwrought expression of love for this girl unless one understands that, for Dante, Beatrice was an idol and, as such, a vehicle for his youthful experimentations in poetic expression. Dante was part of the school of Bolognese poet Guido Calvalcanti whose *dolce stil nuovo* (the sweet new style) made him famous. What was new in the style was its self-conscious attempt to create an Italian poetry, following in the footsteps of the Provencal troubadours and the Sicilians.

The subject of the *Vita Nuova* is, as the title suggests, the new life that has opened up to the young Dante. That new life is, first of all, the life of love, idealized love for a woman as expressed in poetry. It draws heavily on the tradition of courtly love prevalent at the time. For the Provencal troubadours who were members of a court, love for a fair lady, most often the wife of another man, was a constant subject of their songs. Idealizing the woman from a distance, the troubadour would have to content himself with no physical display of his affections. His love was passionate yet never consummated. He preferred to examine the whole range of emotions associated with the powerful surges of infatuation and idealized love to the actual experience of erotic bodily contact. He was gallant and virtuous in his self-control. His love for the lady was a secret that only he and his beloved shared. He would find consolation in no other out of faithfulness to his lady.

The new life Dante discovered is also the life of the mind and creative, artistic expression. The young Florentine found its consolations every bit as pleasing as those of a woman. In fact, they were more so, because they are capable of limitless satisfaction, once one makes the passage from the world of externals to the interior world of the soul. Whereas the person dependent on the senses must be content with the inevitable disappointment that comes from reliance on others, the self-motivated can find contentment in the realm of the ideal.

Dante, along with his fellows in the school of Calvalcanti, styled himself a *fedele d'amore,* a liege of love, whose dedication to ideal love would overcome every hardship.

THE *COMMEDIA*

Dante began his great work, the *Commedia,* during the winds and storms of midlife. What made his political downfall so bitter was that it came as the result of treachery. The pope himself, the vicar of Christ on earth, had deceived those loyal to him. His intervention and the willingness of Dante and the rest of the Signoria to work for peace with the Blacks had led to their utter defeat, which meant the loss of their power, their property, their freedom and, in some cases, their lives.

There was nowhere for Dante to go. He couldn't move into city government somewhere else. The anger and bitterness, the disillusion and despair pushed him back to his literary work, to the new life that he had begun to experience before his political career diverted his energies. The blackness of his failure found its expression in the opening line of the *Commedia:* "When, at mid-life, I had wandered from the straight path, I found myself in a dark wood." "When I had wandered…." Dante blamed himself for failure. His vision was never less than clear. He saw his own failure, as well as the treachery of his enemies, as moral failings. They were sins, departures from the right way, brought about by choosing bad over good, by forgetting the moral basics, by turning aside.

His downfall was the result of vice working in human affairs. To understand it, he had to examine the actions of evil, not only in his enemies, but in himself as well. He had stopped listening to the voice of conscience that told him that the glamor of politics has another, darker side. He had felt it when he had exiled his cousin, Corso di Donati. If only he had turned from the falseness earlier. If only he had chosen to pursue the life that had opened to him in the writing of the *Vita Nuova* and not become so distracted by the tinsel of public life.

To capture this in literature, he needed an imaginative framework to handle a subject as large as the effect of vice and virtue on human affairs. He constructed a cosmic epic that begins with a descent into the center of the earth and ends beyond our solar system in outer space. He examines vice in exquisite detail. Each of the seven deadly sins are displayed in their effects upon the soul's health. At the same time Dante revenged the dishonor he received in Florence. He vented his anger, showing his enemies for what they were—morally bankrupt—and illustrated their ultimate damnation.

The *Commedia* has three sections: the famous opening book, the *Inferno;* the masterful *Purgatorio;* and the little-read conclusion, *Paradiso.* The poem is carefully structured with nothing left to chance. Dante tries to replicate the order of the divinely created universe in his own work. Each book has thirty-three cantos. The first serves as an introduction to the entire work, making a total of one hundred, a number that, to Dante's medieval readers, signified the square root of the perfect number: ten. Ten was the square of the trinitarian number three, plus one, the number of divine unity. The rhyme of the poem is the "third rhyme," the *terza rima* that Dante invented especially for this work, reflecting the trinitarian number.

It is written in Italian, rather than Latin, the language of scholarship. Dante had experimented with that style as a *fedele d'amore* and now when he wished to create a story that grew out of the realities of Florentine life, he chose the language of the people. In doing so he used his native Italian to its fullest, even inventing new words and expressions when the existing language was unable to express his otherworldly visions. So significant was the impact of the *Commedia* that Dante's Florentine dialect became the basis for modern Italian.

The *Commedia* is an epic poem. It employs sound to create its effects in a way that is simply not translatable out of Italian. If it were simply a masterpiece of aural craft, however, few non-Italian speakers would know of it today. But Dante's poem is so much more than simply a treat to the ear. It is, first of all, a great story. At every turn we are moved briskly through the narrative by fantastic action. As Dante descends into the Inferno he meets souls of the damned eating one another's flesh, baked by fire, and sunken to their heads in human waste. He encounters monsters, demons, and at the bottom of the pit, he must struggle to escape by climbing over the back of Satan himself, frozen in the lake of Dis, beating his batlike wings pointlessly trying to escape.

In Purgatory, Dante climbs a seven-story mountain, battling on each level one of the seven deadly sins. At the final stage, he passes out of this world into an intergalactic adventure, moving from the earth through eight planets to the region beyond, where God dwells.

Action is blended with rich, unforgettable visual imagery. Judas Iscariot is chewed in one of the mouths of Satan for all eternity. Dido is locked in her lover's arms forever—punishment by unlimited granting of the adulterers' lust. In the earthly paradise, which sits above the seven-story mountain of Purgatory, Beatrice appears to Dante in a regal procession, riding in a chariot drawn by a griffin. As Dante watches spellbound, the scene of heavenly beauty is suddenly destroyed as a dragon ascending from below the earth smashes through the floor of the cart.

The *Commedia* is not only a great story, it is an epic story. True to that form it is about a journey. Throughout Western religion, the spiritual life is often depicted as a journey from one place to another. Abraham is told to travel from his homeland in Ur of the Caldees to a land that God will show him. Moses leads the Israelites out of Egypt into the desert where for forty years they travel to the Promised Land. Mohammed flees Mecca in 622 and begins to gather a following. Jesus goes about healing and freeing those possessed by the devil, charging his disciples to likewise lead lives of itinerant preachers.

Christian writers picked up the idea. John Climacus talked about the progress of the spiritual life as climbing a ladder. Bonaventure, who died when Dante was nine, wrote *The Soul's Journey into God.* After Dante, the Protestant English-speaking world received its own reflection of this in Bunyan's *Pilgrim's Progress.* Columbus saw his journey to the New World as a spiritual passage ushering in the final Third Age of the Holy Spirit.

All of this highlights the fact that the *Commedia* is an allegory. Dante presents the leading character of the drama as a traveler, a Pilgrim. The Pilgrim is both Dante Alighieri, wandering through a world where he finds his old Florentine associates, and Everyman, facing the forces of good and evil as they battle for his soul. The symbolism of the poem is intricate and carefully developed, drawing on both classical and Christian sources. Virgil, Dante's guide in *Inferno* and *Purgatorio,* is the symbol of reason. The she-wolf that threatens to devour Dante is a symbol of lust, and the lion stalking him is pride. The reed with which the Pilgrim girds himself on the shores of the mount of Purgatory stands for humility, and the enchanting figure of Beatrice, as we shall see, for human and divine love.

Love Misdirected

Virgil tells Dante as they travel along the level of Purgatory where the Slothful struggle:

> It should be clear to you by now how blind to truth those
> people are who make the claims that every love is, in itself,
> good love. (*Purgatorio* xviii, 34)

To a generation that grew up singing "all you need is love" and heard preached "God is love" and little else, it is hard to conceive that not every love is good love. Some men love women they meet in bars. Some love the way alcohol makes them feel. Others love overeating. But in each case those loves are misdirected. They are loves of things that are not always bad in themselves but become bad in the lives of the people pursuing them because they divert them from loving the highest good. Lesser loves, loves that cannot satisfy the soul for long, become bad when they displace the highest good from its rightful place in the soul. In such cases love becomes lust: desiring things more than we should and more than the things in themselves merit. We place an idol in the place of the ultimate good and lust after it. In our effort to force this love to become something it cannot be, we deceive ourselves. The more reality demonstrates our folly, the more lust clings until it is, as Kierkegaard so rightly noted in his "Diary of a Seducer," an act of utter desperation.

Misdirected love condemns a soul to the Inferno. Dante places the lustful in the second of the nine circles of Hell. Theirs is the mildest of the torments of Hell proper. Yet this is no place of pleasures. It is completely unlike the first circle of Hell, Limbo, in which righteous pagan souls like Virgil reside. It is a place of anguish where "storm and counterstorm through time foregone, sweep the souls of the damned before its charge, whirling and battering it drives them on." As they are constantly buffeted by the wind, which, like their lusts, compels them and clouds their vision, they cry out blaspheming the power of God. They are without hope in the world of the damned. There Dido, Tristan, Cleopatra, and Helen are joined by countless throngs of hapless souls.

In Purgatory there are likewise those whose misdirected love has led them astray, but to a significantly lesser degree. Purgatory is an island mountain. All who have called upon the name of the Lord have been saved. But each soul must perfect itself by climbing the mountain to be made more perfect before approaching Paradise. Purgatory is a land in which "souls whose loves are bad" labor. There are the proud, who loved themselves too much; the envious who loved the goods of others too much; the wrathful who loved their own ways too much. There are those also who loved too little: the slothful whose tepidity prevented them from entering the fullness of the Kingdom of God. And there are those whose misdirected loves were excessive, distorting their judgment and turning them away: the lustful, the gluttonous, and the avaricious, and prodigal.

In Canto XIX, the Pilgrim is sleeping peacefully when he sees a woman in a dream. At first he perceives her as exceedingly ugly and revolting. But as he looks longer his eyes "worked upon her to free her tongue and straighten out all her deformities." He finds himself enchanted with the hag, projecting upon her a beauty that he desires, beguiled by her Siren's song to see her as something she is not. Virgil then appears and rips open her shirt exposing her ugly, rotting flesh. The stench brings the Pilgrim to his senses as Virgil tells him: "You saw that ageless sorceress for whom alone the souls above must weep; you saw also how men escape from her" (XIX.12.53).

The Will To Rise

The *Commedia* is a journey from death to life. It begins with a descent, a *katabasis*. Just as Job had to fall before rising, so also the Pilgrim. When he wishes to escape the she-wolf and lion that assail him in the dark wood, he is told by Virgil: "he must go by another way who would escape this wilderness." That way is down into the Inferno. Only by confronting the consequences of sin—sin that comes near to devouring him— can the Pilgrim be saved. The process of descent into the abyss is the beginning of a cleansing of the will, a reordering of the energies of the soul from lesser goods to the highest good. Only by thus purging the will and freeing it can a soul be redeemed. Virgil tells the Pilgrim: "The will to rise alone proves purity; once freed, it takes possession of the soul and wills the soul to change its company" (XXI.61).

This will to rise must carry the Pilgrim out of the Inferno, through the most horrible of all routes—over the back of Satan himself. It is that will that Cato speaks of when he meets the Pilgrim on the shores of Purgatory and wishes that "the lamp that lights your upward path find in your will enough sustaining fuel to take you to the enameled mountain top."

Purgatory is a mountain that heals all who climb it. Each soul progresses at its own speed. The Pilgrim receives seven *p*'s on his forehead, one for each of the deadly sins. He must have each of them removed as he climbs. The horrible sights that so terrified him in Hell no longer haunt and paralyze him. He bathes in the river Lethe, the river of forgetfulness, which separates the Inferno from Purgatory. He forgets the despair of Hell, the obsession with one's own guilt that dominates the conscience of the damned. And he forgets the hopelessness that clouds the air of the Inferno. As soon as he lands on the island of Purgatory he notices that the atmosphere is different. There is light and there is air. It is an arduous place, but a place where effort brings freedom and new life.

Love Rightly Ordered

As the Pilgrim climbs the mountain he is increasingly compelled to do so by love. With each step he finds himself getting lighter. As he removes the *p*'s from his forehead, he becomes more enthused about continuing. The love that motivates him is a love of the good, rightly ordered. Virgil says of this love that "just as much ardor as it finds, it gives" (XV.70).

When the Pilgrim has climbed to the highest point of the mountain and has gone through the final trial, Virgil leaves him with these words that sum up the whole meaning of the ascent: "Now is your will upright, wholesome and free, and not to heed its pleasure would be wrong." What a metamorphosis has taken place. The will perverted to lust at the lower levels kept one from rising. Now it is upright and must be followed. The good can be loved only by one whose will is truly free to do so. Loving is ultimately a

function of the will, the will freed from lust and able to respond to
the love that comes forth from God himself.

When he at last reaches Paradise, he is thrilled by the spectacle of a heaven in which each creature is positioned closer to or
further from the divine majesty, according to its nature and its
capacity. Every creature is perfectly happy there. None wants more
than it has. The dynamic of wanting and not having, of being
unfulfilled, is entirely lacking in Paradise. All are content in their
own natures and in God's perfect will.

Here God's will is all and all. There is no distance between
what God wills and what a creature wants. In Dante's memorable
verse:

> In his will is our peace—it is the sea in which all things are
> drawn that it itself creates or which the work of nature
> makes." (*Paradiso,* III.85).

Ultimately Dante's view of human nature is supremely optimistic. Our being is capable of loving the good, capable, when perfected, of responding fully to the love of God. That love comes to
us in many ways. To understand just how, we must look at the figure of Beatrice.

Beatrice

Beatrice, Dante's childhood sweetheart who died an untimely
death in her early twenties, plays a major role in the *Commedia*. It is
Beatrice who leaves Paradise and visits Virgil in Limbo to beg him
to go to Dante and lead him back onto the straight path. Beatrice's
memory compels Dante to endure the trials of the Inferno and
especially of Purgatory. On the final level of the mountain, he must
pass through a wall of flames. Suddenly, all ardor that he possessed
during his climb is gone, and he is afraid of the fire that tempers the
lustful at that last level below the Earthly Paradise. Virgil rouses him
with the promise that Beatrice awaits him on the other side. In the

flames Virgil calls out Beatrice's name to the suffering Pilgrim. As
the Pilgrim enters the Earthly Paradise he sees Beatrice for the first
time since her earthly life ended. As he gazes on her, her eyes in
turn fixed on God, he tells us:

> Gazing upon her I felt myself becoming what Glaucus had
> become tasting the herb that made him like the other sea-
> gods there. Transhumanize—it cannot be explained *per verba,*
> so let this example serve until God's grace grants the experi-
> ence. (*Paradiso* I.67)

As Dante travels on with her, he feels that process accelerating in
him. "What I had loved the most of all, things that were not she, I
hated now the most" (XXXI.15).

Beatrice is a symbol of divine love. A wisdom figure who
chides Dante upon their first meeting for turning from the true
way, she instructs him later in his journey. But she is more than
that. She is also a real woman. It is Dante's genius to hold the
human and the divine together in one real, particular person. He
will not let love be idealized to the point where we deal with eternal forms or disembodied muses. Neither will he see in Beatrice
only the gentle little girl he once knew who made him feel warm
inside. She is both love that is sensual, human, even erotic, and love
that is transcendent, purifying, divine. At one point when Dante at
last sees Christ, he cannot take his eyes off Beatrice (to her great
consternation). The two cannot be easily separated.

She is all that and she is also the only way that Dante can
enter Paradise. After he has completed his ascent of the mountain,
he finds his guide Virgil has disappeared. Reason can lead him no
further. He is now in the realm where only love can penetrate the
cloud of unknowing that surrounds the Most High. Only a perfect
love can bring one into the presence of perfect love itself. Dante is
saying in the most sublime way that transcendence cannot be
attained by ignoring the incarnate reality of other persons. It is in
contact with them, it is in loving them that we are lifted up, "trans-
humanized," divinized, filled with the divine nature.

Such a statement clearly is a mark of an age when the immanence of God, as incarnate in the human Christ, was very much a concern. What we see in St. Francis of Assisi's devotion to the humanity of Christ, we see in Dante as well, even though the forms in which the two writers express it are distinct.

Dante Today

Today there is so much confusion about love. Dante is a prophet to our age. His message is that the love we often seek in others can in fact be all that we hope it might be, precisely because it is not only what we think it is—it is not only the love of that person—but the very love of God. In that particular experience of love the universe can open to us. We sense that, and it is what makes love so exciting.

But only when love is rightly ordered can it rise to its highest, most fulfilling levels. For that to happen, one must not only love his Beatrice but one must love the One whom Beatrice loves and Who shines in her eyes. The highest good must be loved for what it is; Beatrice for what she is. Any other scheme will fail, will confuse us and ultimately bring us down. Without the love of the highest good, Beatrice is called upon to do too much, to meet our every practical need and to respond to that never-healing wound within us that only transcendence will soothe. Without the love of the Highest, Beatrice is called upon to do too little, for she is only a human being with an aging body and an imperfect ability to please us. But with that love our personal Beatrice can grant us a glimmer, a foretaste of the love that Dante said "moves the sun and other stars."

BIBLIOGRAPHY

Auerbach, Erich. *Dante, Poet of the Secular World*. Trans. Ralph Manheim. Chicago, 1961.

Brandeis, Irma. *The Ladder of Vision: A Study of Dante's Comedy*. New York, 1961.

Eliot, T. S. *Dante*. London, 1929.

Fergusson, Francis. *Dante*. New York, 1966.

Pound, Ezra. *The Spirit of Romance*. London, 1910.

INFERNO[6]

CANTO I

Midway upon the journey of our life
    I found myself within a forest dark,
    For the straightforward pathway had been lost.
Ah me! how hard a thing it is to say
    What was this forest savage, rough, and stern,
    Which in the very thought renews the fear.
So bitter is it, death is little more;
    But of the good to treat, which there I found,
    Speak will I of the other things I saw there.
I cannot well repeat how there I entered,
    So full was I of slumber at the moment
    In which I had abandoned the true way.
But after I had reached a mountain's foot,
    At that point where the valley terminated,
    Which had with consternation pierced my heart,
Upward I looked, and I beheld its shoulders,
    Vested already with that planet's rays
    Which leadeth others right by every road.
Then was the fear a little quieted
    That in my heart's lake had endured throughout
    The night, which I had passed so piteously.
And even as he, who, with distressful breath,
    Forth issued from the sea upon the shore,
    Turns to the water perilous and gazes;
So did my soul, that still was fleeing onward,
    Turn itself back to re-behold the pass
    Which never yet a living person left.

---

6. *The Divine Comedy of Dante Alighieri,* trans. Henry Wadsworth Longfellow (New York: Houghton, Mifflin and Company, 1895).

After my weary body I had rested,
　　The way resumed I on the desert slope,
　　So that the firm foot ever was the lower.
And lo! almost where the ascent began,
　　A panther light and swift exceedingly,
　　Which with a spotted skin was covered o'er!
And never moved she from before my face,
　　Nay, rather did impede so much my way,
　　That many times I to return had turned.
The time was the beginning of the morning,
　　And up the sun was mounting with those stars
　　That with him were, what time the Love Divine
At first in motion set those beauteous things;
　　So were to me occasion of good hope,
　　The variegated skin of that wild beast,
The hour of time, and the delicious season;
　　But not so much, that did not give me fear
　　A lion's aspect which appeared to me.
He seemed as if against me he were coming
　　With head uplifted, and with ravenous hunger,
　　So that it seemed the air was afraid of him;
And a she-wolf, that with all hungerings
　　Seemed to be laden in her meagreness,
　　And many folk has caused to live forlorn!
She brought upon me so much heaviness,
　　With the affright that from her aspect came,
　　That I the hope relinquished of the height.
And as he is who willingly acquires,
　　And the time comes that causes him to lose,
　　Who weeps in all his thoughts and is despondent,
E'en such made me that beast withouten peace,
　　Which, coming on against me by degrees
　　Thrust me back thither where the sun is silent.
While I was rushing downward to the lowland,
　　Before mine eyes did one present himself,
　　Who seemed from long-continued silence hoarse.
When I beheld him in the desert vast,
　　"Have pity on me," unto him I cried,
　　"Whiche'er thou art, or shade or real man!"

He answered me: "Not man; man once I was,
    And both my parents were of Lombardy,
    And Mantuans by country both of them.
Sub Julio was I born, though it was late,
    And lived at Rome under the good Augustus,
    During the time of false and lying gods.
A poet was I, and I sang that just
    Son of Anchises, who came forth from Troy,
    After that Ilion the superb was burned.
But thou, why goest thou back to such annoyance?
    Why climb'st thou not the Mount Delectable,
    Which is the source and cause of every joy?"
Now, art thou that Virgilius and that fountain
    Which spreads abroad so wide a river of speech?
    I made response to him with bashful forehead.
"O, of the other poets honour and light,
    Avail me the long study and great love
    That have impelled me to explore thy volume!
Thou art my master, and my author thou,
    Thou art alone the one from whom I took
    The beautiful style that has done honour to me.
Behold the beast, for which I have turned back;
    Do thou protect me from her, famous Sage,
    For she doth make my veins and pulses tremble."
"Thee it behoves to take another road,"
    Responded he, when he beheld me weeping,
    "If from this savage place thou wouldst escape;
Because this beast, at which thou criest out,
    Suffers not any one to pass her way,
    But so doth harass him, that she destroys him;
And has a nature so malign and ruthless,
    That never doth she glut her greedy will,
    And after food is hungrier than before.
Many the animals with whom she weds,
    And more they shall be still, until the Greyhound
    Comes, who shall make her perish in her pain.

He shall not feed on either earth or pelf,
    But upon wisdom, and on love and virtue;
    'Twixt Feltro and Feltro shall his nation be;
Of that low Italy shall he be the saviour,
    On whose account the maid Camilla died,
    Euryalus, Turnus, Nisus, of their wounds;
Through every city shall he hunt her down,
    Until he shall have driven her back to Hell,
    There from whence envy first did let her loose.
Therefore I think and judge it for thy best
    Thou follow me, and I will be thy guide,
    And lead thee hence through the eternal place,
Where thou shalt hear the desperate lamentations,
    Shalt see the ancient spirits disconsolate,
    Who cry out each one for the second death;
And thou shalt see those who contented are
    Within the fire, because they hope to come,
    Whene'er it may be, to the blessed people.
To whom, then, if thou wishest to ascend,
    A soul shall be for that than I more worthy;
    With her at my departure I will leave thee;
Because that Emperor, who reigns above,
    In that I was rebellious to his law,
    Wills that through me none come into his city.
He governs everywhere, and there he reigns;
    There is his city and his lofty throne;
    O happy he whom thereto he elects!"
And I to him: "Poet, I thee entreat,
    By that same God whom thou didst never know,
    So that I may escape this woe and worse,
Thou wouldst conduct me there where thou hast said,
    That I may see the portal of Saint Peter,
    And those thou makest so disconsolate."
Then he moved on, and I behind him followed.

CANTO XXXIV

"Vexilla Regis prodeunt Inferni
    Towards us; therefore look in front of thee,"
    My Master said, "if thou discernest him."
As, when there breathes a heavy fog, or when
    Our hemisphere is darkening into night,
    Appears far off a mill the wind is turning,
Methought that such a building then I saw;
    And, for the wind, I drew myself behind
    My Guide, because there was no other shelter.
Now was I, and with fear in verse I put it,
    There where the shades were wholly covered up,
    And glimmered through like unto straws in glass.
Some prone are lying, others stand erect,
    This with the head, and that one with the soles;
    Another, bow-like, face to feet inverts.
When in advance so far we had proceeded,
    That it my Master pleased to show to me
    The creature who once had the beauteous semblance,
He from before me moved and made me stop,
    Saying: "Behold Dis, and behold the place
    Where thou with fortitude must arm thyself."
How frozen I became and powerless then,
    Ask it not, Reader, for I write it not,
    Because all language would be insufficient.
I did not die, and I alive remained not;
    Think for thyself now, hast thou aught of wit,
    What I became, being of both deprived.
The Emperor of the kingdom dolorous
    From his mid-breast forth issued from the ice;
    And better with a giant I compare
Than do the giants with those arms of his;
    Consider now how great must be that whole,
    Which unto such a part conforms itself.
Were he as fair once, as he now is foul,
    And lifted up his brow against his Maker,
    Well may proceed from him all tribulation.

O, what a marvel it appeared to me,
    When I beheld three faces on his head!
    The one in front, and that vermilion was;
Two were the others, that were joined with this
    Above the middle part of either shoulder.
    And they were joined together at the crest;
And the right-hand one seemed 'twixt white and yellow;
    The left was such to look upon as those
    Who come from where the Nile falls valley-ward.
Underneath each came forth two might wings,
    Such as befitting were so great a bird;
    Sails of the sea I never saw so large.
No feathers had they, but as of a bat
    Their fashion was; and he was waving them,
    So that three winds proceeded forth therefrom.
Thereby Cocytus wholly was congealed.
    With six eyes did he weep, and down three chins
    Trickled the tear-drops and the bloody drivel.
At every mouth he with his teeth was crunching
    A sinner, in the manner of a brake,
    So that he three of them tormented thus.
To him in front the biting was as naught
    Unto the clawing, for sometimes the spine
    Utterly stripped of all the skin remained.
"That soul up there which has the greatest pain,"
    The Master said, "is Judas Iscariot;
    With head inside, he plies his legs without.
Of the two others, who head downward are,
    The one who hangs from the black jowl is Brutus;
    See how he writhes himself, and speaks no word.
And the other, who so stalwart seems, is Cassius.
    But night is reascending, and 'tis time
    That we depart, for we have seen the whole."
As seemed him good, I clasped him round the neck,
    And he the vantage seized of time and place,
    And when the wings were opened wide apart,

He laid fast hold upon the shaggy sides;
    From fell to fell descended downward then
    Between the thick hair and the frozen crust.
When we were come to where the thigh revolves
    Exactly on the thickness of the haunch,
    The Guide, with labour and with hard-drawn breath,
Turned round his head where he had had his legs,
    And grappled to the hair, as one who mounts,
    So that to Hell I thought we were returning.
"Keep fast thy hold, for by such stairs as these,"
    The Master said, panting as one fatigued,
    "must we perforce depart from so much evil."
Then through the opening of a rock he issued,
    And down upon the margin seated me;
    Then tow'rds me he outstretched his wary step.
I lifted up mine eyes and thought to see
    Lucifer in the same way I had left him;
    And I beheld him upward hold his legs.
And if I then became disquieted,
    Let stolid people think who do not see
    What the point is beyond which I had passed.
"Rise up," the Master said, "upon thy feet;
    The way is long, and difficult the road,
    And now the sun to middle-tierce returns."
It was not any palace corridor
    There where we were, but dungeon natural,
    With floor uneven and unease of light.
"E're from the abyss I tear myself away,
    "My Master," said I when I had arisen,
    "To draw me from an error speak a little;
Where is the ice? and how is this one fixed
    Thus upside down? And how in such short time
    From eve to morn has the sun made his transit?"
And he to me: "Thou still imaginest
    Thou art beyond the centre, where I grasped
    The hair of the fell worm, who mines the world.

That side thou wast, so long as I descended;
    When round I turned me, thou didst pass the point
    To which things heavy draw from every side,
And now beneath the hemisphere art come
    Opposite that which overhangs the vast
    Dry-land, and 'neath whose cope was put to death
The Man who without sin was born and lived.
    Thou hast thy feet upon the little sphere
    Which makes the other face of the Judecca.
Here it is morn when it is evening there;
    And he who with his hair a stairway made us
    Still fixed remaineth as he was before.
Upon this side he fell down out of heaven;
    And all the land, that whilom here emerged,
    For fear of him made of the sea a veil,
And came to our hemisphere; and peradventure
    To flee from him, what on this side appears
    Left the place vacant here, and back recoiled."
A place there is below, from Beelzebub
    As far receding as the tomb extends,
    Which not by sight is known, but by the sound
Of a small rivulet, that there descendeth
    Through chasm within the stone, which it has gnawed
    With course that winds about and slightly falls.
The Guide and I into that hidden road
    Now entered, to return to the bright world;
    And without care of having any rest
We mounted up, he first and I the second,
    Till I beheld through a round aperture
    Some of the beauteous things that Heaven doth bear;
Thence we came forth to rebehold the stars.

PURGATORIO

CANTO I

To run o'er better waters hoists its sail
    The little vessel of my genius now,
    That leaves behind itself a sea so cruel;
And of that second kingdom will I sing
    Wherein the human spirit doth purge itself,
    And to ascend to heaven becometh worthy.
Let dead Poesy here rise again,
    O holy Muses, since that I am yours,
    And here Calliope somewhat ascend,
My song accompanying with that sound,
    Of which the miserable magpies felt
    The blow so great, that they despaired of pardon.
Sweet colour of the oriental sapphire,
    That was upgathered in the cloudless aspect
    Of the pure air, as far as the first circle,
Unto mine eyes did recommence delight
    Soon as I issued forth from the dead air,
    Which had with sadness filled mine eyes and breast.
The beauteous planet, that to love incites,
    Was making all the orient to laugh,
    Veiling the Fishes that were in her escort.
To the right hand I turned, and fixed my mind
    Upon the other pole, and saw four stars
    Ne'er seen before save by the primal people.
Rejoicing in their flamelets seemed the heaven.
    O thou septentrional and widowed site,
    Because thou art deprived of seeing these!
When from regarding them I had withdrawn,
    Turning a little to the other pole,
    There where the Wain had disappeared already,

I saw beside me an old man alone,
     Worthy of so much reverence in his look,
     That more owes not to father any son.
A long beard and with white hair intermingled
     He wore, in semblance like unto the tresses,
     Of which a double list fell on his breast.
The rays of the four consecrated stars
     Did so adorn his countenance with light,
     That him I saw as were the sun before him.
"Who are you? ye who, counter the blind river,
     Have fled away from the eternal prison?"
     Moving those venerable plumes, he said:
"Who guided you? or who has been your lamp
     In issuing forth out of the night profound,
     That ever black makes the infernal valley?
The laws of the abyss, are they thus broken?
     Or is there changed in heaven some council new,
     That being damned ye come unto my crags?"
Then did my Leader lay his grasp upon me,
     And with his words, and with his hands and signs,
     Reverent he made in me my knees and brow.
Then answered him: "I came not of myself;
     A Lady from Heaven descended, at whose prayers
     I aided this one with my company.
But since it is thy will more be unfolded
     Of our condition, how it truly is,
     Mine cannot be that this should be denied thee.
This one has never his last evening seen,
     But by his folly was so near to it
     That very little time was there to turn.
As I have said, I unto him was sent
     To rescue him, and other way was none
     Than this to which I have myself betaken.
I've shown him all the people of perdition,
     And now those spirits I intend to show
     Who purge themselves beneath thy guardianship.

How I have brought him would be long to tell thee.
    Virtue descendeth from on high that aids me
    To lead him to behold thee and to hear thee.
Now may it please thee to vouchsafe his coming;
    He seeketh Liberty, which is so dear,
    As knoweth he who life for her refuses.
Thou know'st it; since, for her, to thee not bitter
    Was death in Utica, where thou didst leave
    The vesture, that will shine so, the great day.
By us the eternal edicts are not broken;
    Since this one lives, and Minos binds not me;
    But of that circle I, where are the chaste
Eyes of thy Marcia, who in looks still prays thee,
    O holy breast, to hold her as thine own;
    For her love, then, incline thyself to us.
Permit us through thy sevenfold realm to go;
    I will take back this grace from thee to her,
    If to be mentioned there below thou deignest."
"Marcia so pleasing was unto mine eyes
    While I was on the other side," then said he,
    "That every grace she wished of me I granted;
Now that she dwells beyond the evil river,
    She can no longer move me, by that law
    Which, when I issued forth from there, was made.
But if a Lady of Heaven do move and rule thee,
    As thou dost say, no flattery is needful;
    Let it suffice thee that for her thou ask me.
Go, then, and see thou gird this one about
    With a smooth rush, and that thou wash his face,
    So that thou cleanse away all stain therefrom,
For 'twere not fitting that the eye o'ercast
    By any mist should go before the first
    Angel, who is of those of Paradise.
This little island round about its base
    Below there, yonder, where the billow beats it,
    Doth rushes bear upon its washy ooze;

No other plant that putteth forth the leaf,
    Or that doth indurate, can there have life,
    Because it yieldeth not unto the shocks.
Thereafter be not this way your return;
    The sun, which now is rising, will direct you
    To take the mount by easier ascent."
With this he vanished; and I raised me up
    Without a word, and wholly drew myself
    Unto my Guide, and turned mine eyes to him.
And he began: "Son, follow thou my steps;
    Let us turn back, for on this side declines
    The plain unto its lower boundaries."
The dawn was vanquishing the matin hour
    Which fled before it, so that from afar
    I recognised the trembling of the sea.
Along the solitary plain we went
    As one who unto the lost road returns;
    And till he finds it seems to go in vain.
As soon as we were come to where the dew
    Fights with the sun, and, being in a part
    Where shadow falls, little evaporates,
Both of his hands upon the grass outspread
    In gentle manner did my Master place;
    Whence I, who of his action was aware,
Extended unto him my tearful cheeks;
    There did he make in me uncovered wholly
    That hue which Hell had covered up in me.
Then came we down upon the desert shore
    Which never yet saw navigate its waters
    Any that afterward had known return.
There he begirt me as the other pleased;
    O marvellous! for even as he culled
    The humble plant, such it sprang up again
Suddenly there where he uprooted it.

CANTO XV

As much as 'twixt the close of the third hour
    And dawn of day appeareth of that sphere
    Which aye in fashion of a child is playing,
So much it now appeared, towards the night,
    Was of his course remaining to the sun;
    There it was evening, and 'twas midnight here;
And the rays smote the middle of our faces,
    Because by us the mount was so encircled,
    That straight towards the west we now were going
When I perceived my forehead overpowered
    Beneath the splendour far more than at first,
    And stupor were to me the things unknown,
Whereat towards the summit of my brow
    I raised my hands, and made myself the visor
    Which the excessive glare diminishes.
As when from off the water, or a mirror,
    The sunbeam leaps unto the opposite side,
    Ascending upward in the selfsame measure
That it descends, and deviates as far
    From falling of a stone in line direct,
    (As demonstrate experiment and art,)
So it appeared to me that by a light
    Refracted there before me I was smitten;
    On which account my sight was swift to flee.
"What is that, Father sweet, from which I cannot
    So fully screen my sight that it avail me,"
    Said I, "and seems towards us to be moving?"
"Marvel thou not, if dazzle thee as yet
    The family of heaven," he answered me;
    "An angel 'tis, who comes to invite us upward.
Soon will it be, that to behold these things
    Shall not be grievous, but delightful to thee
    As much as nature fashioned thee to feel."
When we had reached the Angel benedight,
    With joyful voice he said: "Here enter in
    To stairway far less steep than are the others."

We mounting were, already thence departed,
    And *"Beati misericordes"* was
    Behind us sung, "Rejoice, thou that o'ercomest!"
My Master and myself, we two alone
    Were going upward, and I thought, in going,
    Some profit to acquire from words of his;
And I to him directed me, thus asking:
    "What did the spirit of Romagna mean,
    Mentioning interdict and partnership?"
Whence he to me: "Of his own greatest failing
    He knows the harm; and therefore wonder not
    If he reprove us, that we less may rue it.
Because are thither pointed your desires
    Where by companionship each share is lessened,
    Envy doth ply the bellows to your sighs.
But if the love of the supernal sphere
    Should upwardly direct your aspiration,
    There would not be a fear within your breast;
For there, as much the more as one says *Our,*
    So much the more of good each one possesses,
    And more of charity in that cloister burns."
"I am more hungering to be satisfied,"
    I said, "than if I had before been silent,
    And more of doubt within my mind I gather.
How can it be, that boon distributed
    The more possessors can more wealthy make
    Therein, than if by few it be possessed?"
And he to me: "Because thou fixest still
    Thy mind entirely upon earthly things,
    Thou pluckest darkness from the very light.
That goodness infinite and ineffable
    Which is above there, runneth unto love,
    As to a lucid body comes the sunbeam.
So much it gives itself as it finds ardour,
    So that as far as charity extends,
    O'er it increases the eternal valour.

And the more people thitherward aspire,

    More are there to love well, and more they love there,

    And, as a mirror, one reflects the other.

And if my reasoning appease thee not,

    Thou shalt see Beatrice; and she will fully

    Take from thee this and every other longing.

Endeavour, then, that soon may be extinct,

    As are the two already, the five wounds

    That close themselves again by being painful."

Even as I wished to say, "Thou dost appease me,"

    I saw that I had reached another circle,

    So that my eager eyes made me keep silence.

There it appeared to me that in a vision

    Ecstatic on a sudden I was rapt,

    And in a temple many persons saw;

And at the door a woman, with the sweet

    Behaviour of a mother, saying: "Son,

    Why in this manner hast thou dealt with us?

Lo, sorrowing, thy father and myself

    Were seeking for thee";—and as here she ceased,

    That which appeared at first had disappeared.

Then I beheld another with those waters

    Adown her cheeks which grief distils whenever

    From great disdain of others it is born,

And saying: "If of that city thou art lord,

    For whose name was such strife among the gods,

    And whence doth every science scintillate,

Avenge thyself on those audacious arms

    That clasped our daughter, O Pisistratus";

    And the lord seemed to me benign and mild

To answer her with aspect temperate:

    "What shall we do to those who wish us ill,

    If he who loves us be by us condemned?"

Then saw I people hot in fire of wrath,

    With stones a young man slaying, clamorously

    Still crying to each other, "Kill him! kill him!"

And him I saw bow down, because of death
    That weighed already on him, to the earth,
    But of his eyes made ever gates to heaven,
Imploring the high Lord, in so great strife,
    That he would pardon those his persecutors,
    With such an aspect as unlocks compassion.
Soon as my soul had outwardly returned
    To things external to it which are true,
    Did I my false errors not recognize.
My Leader, who could see me bear myself
    Like to a man that rouses him from sleep,
    Exclaimed: "What ails thee, that thou canst not stand?
But hast been coming more than half a league
    Veiling thine eyes, and with thy legs entangled,
    In guise of one whom wine or sleep subdues?"
"O my sweet Father, if thou listen to me,
    I'll tell thee," said I, "what appeared to me,
    When thus from me my legs were ta'en away."
And he: "If thou shouldst have a hundred masks
    Upon thy face, from me would not be shut
    Thy cogitations, howsoever small.
What thou hast seen was that thou mayst not fail
    To ope thy heart unto the waters of peace,
    Which from the eternal fountain are diffused.
I did not ask, 'What ails thee?' as he does
    Who only looketh with the eyes that see not
    When of the soul bereft the body lies,
But asked it to give vigour to thy feet;
    Thus must we needs urge on the sluggards, slow
    To use their wakefulness when it returns."
We passed along, athwart the twilight peering
    Forward as far as ever eye could stretch
    Against the sunbeams serotine and lucent;
And lo! by slow degrees a smoke approached
    In our direction, sombre as the night,
    Nor was there place to hide one's self therefrom
This of our eyes and the pure air bereft us.

CANTO XXX

When the Septentrion of the highest heaven
    (Which never either setting knew or rising,
    Nor veil of other cloud than that of sin,
And which made every one therein aware
    Of his own duty, as the lower makes
    Whoever turns the helm to come to port)
Motionless halted, the veracious people,
    That came at first between it and the Griffin,
    Turned themselves to the car, as to their peace.
And one of them, as if by Heaven commissioned,
    Singing, *"Veni, sponsa, de Libano"*
    Shouted three times, and all the others after.
Even as the Blessed at the final summons
    Shall rise up quickened each one from his cavern,
    Uplifting light the reinvested flesh,
So upon that celestial chariot
    A hundred rose *ad vocem tanti senis,*
    Ministers and messengers of life eternal.
They all were saying, *"Benedictus qui venis,"*
    And, scattering flowers above and round about,
    "Manibus o date lilia plenis."
Ere now have I beheld, as day began,
    The eastern hemisphere all tinged with rose,
    And the other heaven with fair serene adorned;
And the sun's face, uprising, overshadowed
    So that by tempering influence of vapours
    For a long interval the eye sustained it;
Thus in the bosom of a cloud of flowers
    Which from those hands angelical ascended,
    And downward fell again inside and out,
Over her snow-white veil with olive cinct
    Appeared a lady under a green mantle,
    Vested in colour of the living flame.
And my own spirit, that already now
    So long a time had been, that in her presence
    Trembling with awe it had not stood abashed,

Without more knowledge having by mine eyes,
    Through occult virtue that from her proceeded
    Of ancient love the mighty influence felt.
As soon as on my vision smote the power
    Sublime, that had already pierced me through
    Ere from my boyhood I had yet come forth,
To the left hand I turned with that reliance
    With which the little child runs to his mother,
    When he has fear, or when he is afflicted,
To say unto Virgilius: "Not a drachm
    Of blood remains in me, that does not tremble;
    I know the traces of the ancient flame."
But us Virgilius of himself deprived
    Had left, Virgilius, sweetest of all fathers,
    Virgilius, to whom I for safety gave me:
Nor whatsoever lost the ancient mother
    Availed my cheeks now purified from dew,
    That weeping they should not again be darkened.
"Dante, because Virgilius has departed
    Do not weep yet, do not weep yet awhile;
    For by another sword thou need'st must weep."
E'en as an admiral, who on poop and prow
    Comes to behold the people that are working
    In other ships, and cheers them to well-doing,
Upon the left hand border of the car,
    When at the sound I turned of my own name,
    Which of necessity is here recorded,
I saw the Lady, who erewhile appeared
    Veiled underneath the angelic festival,
    Direct her eyes to me across the river.
Although the veil, that from her head descended,
    Encircled with the foliage of Minerva,
    Did not permit her to appear distinctly,
In attitude still royally majestic
    Continued she, like unto one who speaks,
    And keeps his warmest utterance in reserve:

"Look at me well; in sooth I'm Beatrice!
    How didst thou deign to come unto the Mountain?
    Didst thou not know that man is happy here?"
Mine eyes fell downward into the clear fountain,
    But, seeing myself therein, I sought the grass,
    So great a shame did weigh my forehead down.
As to the son the mother seems superb,
    So she appeared to me; for somewhat bitter
    Tasteth the savour of severe compassion.
Silent became she, and the Angels sang
    Suddenly, *"In te, Domine, speravi"*:
    But beyond *pedes meos* did not pass.
Even as the snow among the living rafters
    Upon the back of Italy congeals,
    Blown on and drifted by Sclavonian winds,
And then, dissolving, trickles through itself
    Whene'er the land that loses shadow breathes,
    So that it seems a fire that melts a taper;
E'en thus was I without a tear or sigh,
    Before the song of those who sing for ever
    After the music of the eternal spheres.
But when I heard in their sweet melodies
    Compassion for me, more than had they said,
    "O wherefore, lady, dost thou thus upbraid him?"
The ice, that was about my heart congealed,
    To air and water changed, and in my anguish
    Through mouth and eyes came gushing from my breast.
She, on the right-hand border of the car
    Still firmly standing, to those holy beings
    Thus her discourse directed afterwards:
"Ye keep your watch in the eternal day,
    So that nor night nor sleep can steal from you
    One step the ages make upon their path;
Therefore my answer is with greater care,
    That he may hear me who is weeping yonder,
    So that the sin and dole be of one measure.

Not only by the work of those great wheels,
 That destine every seed unto some end,
 According as the stars are in conjunction,
But by the largess of celestial graces,
 Which have such lofty vapours for their rain
 That near to them our sight approaches not,
Such had this man become in his new life
 Potentially, that every righteous habit
 Would have made admirable proof in him;
But so much more malignant and more savage
 Becomes the land untilled and with bad seed,
 The more good earthly vigour it possesses.
Some time did I sustain him with my look;
 Revealing unto him my youthful eyes,
 I led him with me turned in the right way.
As soon as ever of my second age
 I was upon the threshold and changed life,
 Himself from me he took and gave to others.
When from the flesh to spirit I ascended,
 And beauty and virtue were in me increased,
 I was to him less dear and less delightful;
And into ways untrue he turned his steps,
 Pursuing the false images of good,
 That never any promises fulfil;
Nor prayer for inspiration me availed,
 By means of which in dreams and otherwise
 I called him back, so little did he heed them.
So low he fell, that all appliances
 For his salvation were already short,
 Save showing him the people of perdition.
For this I visited the gates of death,
 And unto him, who so far up has led him,
 My intercessions were with weeping borne.
God's lofty fiat would be violated,
 If Lethe should be passed, and if such viands
 Should tasted be, withouten any scot
Of penitence, that gushes forth in tears."

PARADISO

CANTO I

The glory of Him who moveth everything
    Doth penetrate the universe, and shine
    In one part more and in another less.
Within that heaven which most his light receives
    Was I, and things beheld which to repeat
    Nor knows, nor can, who from above descends;
Because in drawing near to its desire
    Our intellect ingulphs itself so far,
    That after it the memory cannot go.
Truly whatever of the holy realm
    I had the power to treasure in my mind
    Shall now become the subject of my song.
O good Apollo, for this last emprise
    Make of me such a vessel of thy power
    As giving the beloved laurel asks!
One summit of Parnassus hitherto
    Has been enough for me, but now with both
    I needs must enter the arena left.
Enter into my bosom, thou, and breathe
    As at the time when Marsyas thou didst draw
    Out of the scabbard of those limbs of his.
O power divine, lend'st thou thyself to me
    So that the shadow of the blessed realm
    Stamped in my brain I can make manifest,
Thou'lt see me come unto thy darling tree,
    And crown myself thereafter with those leaves
    Of which the theme and thou shall make me worthy.
So seldom, Father, do we gather them
    For triumph or of Caesar or of Poet,
    (The fault and shame of human inclinations,)

That the Peneian foliage should bring forth
  Joy to the joyous Delphic deity,
    When any one it makes to thirst for it.
A little spark is followed by great flame;
  Perchance with better voices after me
    Shall prayer be made that Cyrrha may respond!
To mortal men by passages diverse
  Uprises the world's lamp; but by that one
    Which circles four uniteth with three crosses,
With better course and with a better star
  Conjoined it issues, and the mundane wax
    Tempers and stamps more after its own fashion.
Almost that passage had made morning there
  And evening here, and there was wholly white
    That hemisphere, and black the other part,
When Beatrice towards the left-hand side
  I saw turned round, and gazing at the sun;
    Never did eagle fasten so upon it!
And even as a second ray is wont
  To issue from the first and reascend,
    Like to a pilgrim who would fain return,
Thus of her action, through the eyes infused
  In my imagination, mine I made,
    And sunward fixed mine eyes beyond our wont.
There much is lawful which is here unlawful
  Unto our powers, by virtue of the place
    Made for the human species as its own.
Not long I bore it, nor so little while
  But I beheld it sparkle round about
    Like iron that comes molten from the fire;
And suddenly it seemed that day to day
  Was added, as if He who has the power
    Had with another sun the heaven adorned.
With eyes upon the everlasting wheels
  Stood Beatrice all intent, and I, on her
    Fixing my vision from above removed,

Such at her aspect inwardly became
    As Glaucus, tasting of the herb that made him
    Peer of the other gods beneath the sea.
To represent transhumanise in words
    Impossible were; the example, then, suffice
    Him for whom Grace the experience reserves.
If I was merely what of me thou newly
    Createdst, Love who governest the heaven,
    Thou knowest, who didst lift me with thy light!
When now the wheel, which thou dost make eternal
    Desiring thee, made me attentive to it
    By harmony thou dost modulate and measure,
Then seemed to me so much of heaven enkindled
    By the sun's flame, that neither rain nor river
    E'er made a lake so widely spread abroad.
The newness of the sound and the great light
    Kindled in me a longing for their cause,
    Never before with such acuteness felt;
Whence she, who saw me as I saw myself,
    To quiet in me my perturbed mind,
    Opened her mouth, ere I did mine to ask,
And she began: "Thou makest thyself so dull
    With false imagining, that thou seest not
    What thou wouldst see if thou hadst shaken it off.
Thou art not upon earth, as thou believest;
    But lightning, fleeing its appropriate site,
    Ne'er ran as thou, who thitherward returnest."
If of my former doubt I was divested
    By these brief little words more smiled than spoken,
    I in a new one was the more ensnared;
And said: "Already did I rest content
    From great amazement; but am now amazed
    In what way I transcend these bodies light."
Whereupon she, after a pitying sigh,
    Her eyes directed tow'rds me with that look
    A mother casts on a delirious child;

And she began:"All things whate'er they be
   Have order among themselves, and this is form,
   That makes the universe resemble God.
Here do the higher creatures see the footprints
   Of the Eternal Power, which is the end
   Whereto is made the law already mentioned.
In the order that I speak of are inclined
   All natures, by their destinies diverse,
   More or less near unto their origin;
Hence they move onward unto ports diverse
   O'er the great sea of being; and each one
   With instinct given it which bears it on.
This bears away the fire towards the moon;
   This is in mortal hearts the motive power
   This binds together and unites the earth.
Nor only the created things that are
   Without intelligence this bow shoots forth,
   But those that have both intellect and love.
The Providence that regulates all this
   Makes with its light the heaven forever quiet,
   Wherein that turns which has the greatest haste.
And thither now, as to a site decreed,
   Bears us away the virtue of that cord
   Which aims its arrows at a joyous mark.
True is it, that as oftentimes the form
   Accords not with the intention of the art,
   Because in answering is matter deaf,
So likewise from this course doth deviate
   Sometimes the creature, who the power possesses,
   Though thus impelled, to swerve some other way,
(In the same wise as one may see the fire
   Fall from a cloud,) if the first impetus
   Earthward is wrested by some false delight.
Thou shouldst not wonder more, if well I judge,
   At thine ascent, than at a rivulet
   From some high mount descending to the lowland.

Marvel it would be in thee, if deprived
    Of hindrance, thou wert seated down below,
    As if on earth the living fire were quiet."
Thereat she heavenward turned again her face.

CANTO XXXII

Absorbed in his delight, that contemplator
    Assumed the willing office of a teacher,
    And gave beginning to these holy words:
"The wound that Mary closed up and anointed,
    She at her feet who is so beautiful,
    She is the one who opened it and pierced it.
Within that order which the third seats make
    Is seated Rachel, lower than the other,
    With Beatrice, in manner as thou seest.
Sarah, Rebecca, Judith, and her who was
    Ancestress of the Singer, who for dole
    Of the misdeed said, *'Miserere mei,'*
Canst thou behold from seat to seat descending
    Down in gradation, as with each one's name
    I through the Rose go down from leaf to leaf.
And downward from the seventh row, even as
    Above the same, succeed the Hebrew women,
    Dividing all the tresses of the flower;
Because, according to the view which Faith
    In Christ had taken, these are the partitions
    By which the sacred stairways are divided.
Upon this side, where perfect is the flower
    With each one of its petals, seated are
    Those who believed in Christ who was to come.
Upon the other side, where intersected
    With vacant spaces are the semicircles,
    Are those who looked to Christ already come.
And as, upon this side, the glorious seat
    Of the Lady of Heaven, and the other seats
    Below it, such a great division make,

So opposite doth that of the great John,
    Who, ever holy, desert and martyrdom
    Endured, and afterwards two years in Hell.
And under him thus to divide were chosen
    Francis, and Benedict, and Augustine,
    And down to us the rest from round to round.
Behold now the high providence divine;
    For one and other aspect of the Faith
    In equal measure shall this garden fill.
And know that downward from that rank which cleaves
    Midway the sequence of the two divisions,
    Not by their proper merit are they seated;
But by another's under fixed conditions;
    For these are spirits one and all assoiled
    Before they any true election had.
Well canst thou recognise it in their faces,
    And also in their voices puerile,
    If thou regard them well and hearken to them.
Now doubtest thou, and doubting thou art silent;
    But I will loosen for thee the strong bond
    In which thy subtile fancies hold thee fast.
Within the amplitude of this domain
    No casual point can possibly find place,
    No more than sadness can, or thirst, or hunger;
For by eternal law has been established
    Whatever thou beholdest, so that closely
    The ring is fitted to the finger here.
And therefore are these people, festinate
    Unto true life, not *sine causa* here
    More and less excellent among themselves.
The King, by means of whom this realm reposes
    In so love and in so great delight
    That no will ventureth to ask for more,
In his own joyous aspect every mind
    Creating, at his pleasure dowers with grace
    Diversely; and let here the effect suffice.

And this is clearly and expressly noted
    For you in Holy Scripture, in those twins
    Who in their mother had their anger roused.
According to the colour of the hair,
    Therefore, with such a grace the light supreme
    Consenteth that they worthily be crowned.
Without, then, any merit of their deeds,
    Stationed are they in different gradations,
    Differing only in their first acuteness.
'Tis true that in the early centuries,
    With innocence, to work out their salvation
    Sufficient was the faith of parents only.
After the earlier ages were completed,
    Behoved it that the males by circumcision
    Unto their innocent wings should virtue add;
But after that the time of grace had come
    Without the baptism absolute of Christ,
    Such innocence below there was retained.
Look now into the face that unto Christ
    Hath most resemblance; for its brightness only
    Is able to prepare thee to see Christ."
On her did I behold so great a gladness
    Rain down, borne onward in the holy minds
    Created through that altitude to fly,
That whatsoever I had seen before
    Did not suspend me in such admiration,
    Nor show me such similitude of God.
And the same Love that first descended there,
    "Ave Maria, gratia plena," singing,
    In front of her his wings expanded wide.
Unto the canticle divine responded
    From every part the court beatified,
    So that each sight became serener for it.
"O holy father, who for me endurest
    To be below here, leaving the sweet place
    In which thou sittest by eternal lot,

Who is the Angel that with so much joy
    Into the eyes is looking of our Queen,
    Enamoured so that he seems made of fire?"
Thus I again recourse had to the teaching
    Of that one who delighted him in Mary
    As doth the star of morning in the sun.
And he to me:"Such gallantry and grace
    As there can be in Angel and in soul,
    All is in him; and thus we fain would have it;
Because he is the one who bore the palm
    Down unto Mary, when the Son of God
    To take our burden on himself decreed.
But now come onward with thine eyes, as I
    Speaking shall go, and note the great patricians
    Of this most just and merciful of empires.
Those two that sit above there most enrapture
    As being very near unto Augusta,
    Are as it were the two roots of this Rose.
He who upon the left is near her placed
    The father is, by whose audacious taste
    The human species so much bitter tastes.
Upon the right thou seest that ancient father
    Of Holy Church, into whose keeping Christ
    The keys committed of this lovely flower.
And he who all the evil days beheld,
    Before his death, of her the beauteous bride
    Who with the spear and with the nails was won,
Beside him sits, and by the other rests
    That leader under whom on manna lived
    The people ingrate, fickle, and stiff-necked.
Opposite Peter seest thou Anna seated,
    So well content to look upon her daughter,
    Her eyes she moves not while she sings Hosanna.
And opposite the eldest household father
    Lucia sits, she who thy Lady moved
    When to rush downward thou didst bend thy brows.
But since the moments of thy vision fly,
    Here will we make full stop, as a good tailor

Who makes the gown according to his cloth,
And unto the first Love will turn our eyes,
   That looking upon Him thou penetrate
   As far as possible through his effulgence.
Truly, lest peradventure thou recede,
   Moving thy wings believing to advance,
   By prayer behoves it that grace be obtained;
Grace from that one who has the power to aid thee;
   And thou shalt follow me with thy affection
   That from my words thy heart turn not aside."
And he began this holy orison.

Chapter 6

RELATING RELIGION AND ART:

BONAVENTURE AND THE ART OF GOD

For many, art is the language of the gods. In it they find beauty and hope. In it they see that their intimate feelings are not theirs alone and thus find transcendence. Some will say they do not believe in God. Few will say they do not believe in art. Music fills our lives more than ever in this electronic age. It is everywhere we go. Drama and theater are part of the average person's daily bread, usually conveyed by the medium of television. The visual arts delight us as well in this age of high-tech design when colors and textures, the likes of which the ancients never knew, abound.

It is often the case that many who are sensitive to art are troubled by religion, or at least by certain aspects of the institution of religion. One friend, who runs a professional theater outside of Washington, D.C., put it this way:

> My art is all about the same things I think religion is about. Everything I do here is aimed at conveying some sense of authentic meaning to people.

Among Evangelical Christians in the United States there has been a significant debate over the role of art in the churches brought about by the popularity of "contemporary Christian" music. That music is, for all intents and purposes, rock and roll. It is indistinguishable in its musical forms from the Top 40. Much of that music carries with it a blatant eroticism and sensualism, which many think has no place in a worship service. Others claim that the forms are neutral and are able to be used to glorify God just a readily as, say, Gregorian chant. Behind the controversy are different views of the relationship of nature and grace. Some believe all of human culture can be utilized in religious worship; others think that only those cultural forms that have been part of a particular tradition are acceptable. The latter think of the traditional cultural forms not as cultural creations at all but as part of the special revelation of the divinity they worship. Evangelicals, as descendants of John Calvin, traditionally have taken a narrow view of what types of cultural creations may be used in worship. They have limited church decoration, for example, when compared to the lavish and ornate decorations found in Orthodox Christianity.

Religion then implies an aesthetic theory, based on theology. It is also true, however, that art implies a certain religious viewpoint. If we leave the narrow definition of religion that limits religion to its institutional dimension and instead think of it as multifaceted in the way Ninian Smart does when he talks about his seven dimensions of religion, then every artistic expression does communicate an implied religious viewpoint. That may include atheism, which is religious in that it makes statements about ultimate questions and addresses fundamental questions that go to the ground of our being.

Many Christians, like those Evangelicals who support the contemporary Christian music program, are searching for a theology that better matches their aesthetic experiences. In some cases their art has brought them a richer and more varied experience of life than their religious theories can account for. At that moment when theory is eclipsed by experience, we may either abandon the project of understanding or attempt to integrate that new experience into our theory. New theories require new tools. Often we become stuck in the thought forms of our own age, imprisoned by the obvious, shackled by the topical. Bonaventure, living eight centuries ago, conceived a breathtaking idea about the relation of art and religion. His notion of Jesus as the Art of God is rich with possibilities for us today.

BONAVENTURE'S LIFE AND TIMES

The question of how to relate religion and art is an ancient one. Plato deals with it briefly in the *Republic*. Christians faced it during the early centuries and argued over it so bitterly that the

Iconoclast controversy in the eighth century was one of the major problems the young church faced.

Christians inherited from Judaism a hatred of idolatry. From the injunctions against graven images in the decalogue to the simplicity of the symbolism and the rituals of the synagogue, there was a distrust of the visual arts. After all, what was to the Jew a graven image was to the Samaritan a work of art. That distrust abided alongside a growing tradition of the visual arts in the church of the first through eighth centuries. During the reign of the Christian ruler Justinian, the controversy reached its apex. Justinian ruled that the Iconoclasts were wrong in their rejection of the new forms of visual imagery used to depict Christ and the saints. The fact that icons were venerated by Christians as windows through which they could enter into the spiritual world was not the equivalent, Justinian held, of worshiping graven images.

The triumph of the Iconophiles was a major boon for arts in the West. It meant that the church could participate both as patroness and as critic in the artistic creations of the society. The Middle Ages were a time when the church become the center of the arts in European society. The church building was transformed from a house or a Roman basilica into a symbolic monument to the creative energies of humanity, joined in a chorus of praise to God. Perhaps the most significant moment in that process came during the first half of the twelfth century in France. There, just outside Paris, Abbot Suger rebuilt the Abbey Church of St. Denis. Funded by the Carolingian king, Abbot Suger wanted to make a statement that would befit the royal person and would give form to the mystical theology of his favorite guide, the Pseudo-Dionysius. Utilizing the new technology of flying buttresses, he produced a soaring, majestic structure. Its airy, seemingly weightless interior focused attention on the ascent to the mysterious realm of darkness in which God dwells. Its strict geometry linked heaven to earth in a way that had never been done before on such a scale.

Soon the Gothic style was copied throughout Europe. The hierarchical system of Dionysius blended perfectly with the concept of the church and the kingdom that both bishops and kings wished to promulgate.

There are, of course, many more examples that could be given. One thinks of the Renaissance, born in Catholic Italy and nurtured in the bosom of the church, or of the great patronage of the arts that has continued to our own day. But the issue that we first engaged still remains. How does the artist think of his act of creation in light of his faith? Here Bonaventure has something to say.

Bonaventure was born around 1217 in the town of Bagnoregio, sixty miles north of Rome near Viterbo. He came from the upper middle class. At seventeen he entered the University of Paris, where he studied theology. He joined the Franciscans and in 1257 was elected minister general at a time when the order was struggling with the controversies between the conventuals and the spirituals. He pursued a middle of the road policy, holding up the model of Francis, whom he had met as a young boy and who was the greatest single inspiration of his life. He died in 1272, was canonized in 1482, and declared a Universal Doctor of the Church.

He has been called the "Teacher of Devotion," a title that expresses the unique blend of piety and intellectual rigor of his works. Some, like Ewert Cousins, have argued that his was the finest synthesis of the mystical thought of the Middle Ages. Bonaventure gave to his own Franciscan spirituality an intellectual vigor its founder lacked and brought the insights of the Little Poor Man of Assisi to the academic world of Paris.

His works are best divided into three periods corresponding with his life. Period one dates from his time as a student and teacher at Paris. The most notable work from this period is his *Commentary on the Sentences of Peter Lombard*. Period two covers his time as minister general. It is the time of his masterpieces on the spiritual life: *The Soul's Journey into God, The Tree of Life, The Triple Way,* and the *Life of Francis*. The final period of his life saw the production of his controversial works, such as his tract against Averroes, the Arab interpreter of Aristotle, entitled *Collations*. For our purposes, it is the work of the second period that is most important.

HIS TEACHING

In his work Bonaventure united three important strands of thought about the spiritual life. The first was the Franciscan idea that creation is a sign and sacrament of God's presence. The second was Augustine's notions that the soul is an image of the Trinity. The third was Pseudo-Dionysius's concept of the emanation of the Godhead through celestial hierarchies.

It was the thought, and perhaps more importantly, the life of Francis that were Bonaventure's constant points of reference as an adult. Francis was born thirty-six years before Bonaventure in 1181 in Assisi. At that time Italy was not a kingdom but a series of city-states, dominated religiously and politically by a strong papacy at Rome. Four popes—Gregory the Great, Alexander III, Innocent III, and Gregory IX—had established the papacy as the most powerful force in Europe, dominating the competing ambitions of secular princes such as Frederick Barbarossa and England's King John.

The story of Francis's life is well known. The son of a wealthy merchant, Francis was a gallant young man who threw himself into enjoying life. After being hospitalized for an injury sustained when fighting in a war against a rival city, he had a series of experiences that convinced him of the futility of his previous way of life. He went on to lead a life of radical discipleship of Christ. Perhaps no other person has ever tried harder to literally fulfill Christ's teachings as they appear in the Gospels. His movement grew quickly, attracting thousands of followers in Italy and throughout Europe.

The heart of Francis's teaching can be seen in his life, rather than in his works, which are limited to a Rule written for his followers, a handful of letters written to his friends, and a few poems, which are praises to God. Had Francis only been an author he certainly would not be remembered today. His work is brief and from a literary standpoint, undistinguished.

But his followers saw in his life a message that they wished to spread abroad. Bonaventure himself played a major role in the production of two lives of Francis that interpreted him in a hagiographic, legendary way. Along with the lives by Thomas of Celano and the work of remembrances of Brother Ugolino, known as the *Fioretti,* these works did more to define the spirituality of Franciscanism than anything.

That spirituality is characterized by a devotion to the humanity of Christ. Francis, as mentioned, radically followed the human example of Jesus. He imitated Jesus in his style of preaching, going out as an itinerant and then sending out his disciplines two by two. He followed him in his manner of life, living with nowhere to lay his head, suffering as he did, even to the point of receiving in his body the stigmata as signs of his crucifixion with Christ. He, in fact, seemed bent on keeping all the hard sayings of Jesus, those hyperbolic challenges that Jesus repeats so often, those prophetic utterances that were all taken to heart quite literally by this man.

Francis's spirituality was also marked by its emphasis on poverty. He called himself *il Poverello,* which means "the little poor one." He personified the virtue of poverty and addressed himself to "Lady Poverty" as a courtier in her service. Beginning the day he stripped himself of his garments in the town center of Assisi before his father and the town magistrates, he rejected totally any sense of private ownership. He refused to take money. He begged for food. He refused gifts of land and livestock.

Poverty was also an important inner disposition. He was poor in spirit. He saw himself as the least of the brethren, the lowest, the most despised. He rejected all forms of honor and status, preferring to be with the lepers and the lame than with the noble. His identification with the downcast of the society—so dramatically portrayed in his kissing of the leper—was total. By realizing his own need for God, he could identify with the needy.

Francis was also known for his awareness of the sacrality and sacramentality of nature. The legends of his talking to animals and his odes to the elements of the earth illustrate a keen sense of the holiness of all of creation. All of nature emanated from one divine source, and as a result, we are linked to it in our innermost being. We all, animate and inanimate, are creations of the same God and, as such, have solidarity. There was no talk of "subduing the earth and conquering it" in Francis. Rather we read, in his *Canticle of Brother Sun:*

> All praise be yours, my Lord, through Sister Earth, our mother,
> Who feeds us in her sovereignty and produces
> Various fruits with colored flowers and herbs.

Creation is not only holy, being made by the Creator, it is also a sacrament: a sign instituted by God to give grace. Hence the things of creation bring blessings to us. For example, again from *Canticle of Brother Sun,* Brother Sun "brings light." Sister Water is "so useful, pure." Brother Fire "brightens the night." And Sister Earth "feeds us." Behind all these blessings is the divine hand, which we can see reflected in them as in a mirror.

This emphasis on creation joins with Francis's devotion to the humanity of Christ. The entire world in which Christ walked becomes sanctified. All of creation takes part in the incarnational union of divine and human. As a result, the creature becomes lovable not only in its essence, but in its finitude and particularity, including, of course, its imperfections. One can love creation not only for God's sake but for its own sake, as well, because that is how it exists for God, who made it to be good and redeemed it in Christ.

Bonaventure takes all of this and applies it to his own work. He gives the new Franciscan spirituality of Creation a place in the traditional mystical theology of his day. In the works of others such as Bernard of Clairvaux, meditation on the earthly life of Christ was profitable but it could be superseded by a purer spiritual union with God that occurred in the rarefied atmosphere of contemplation. Bonaventure emphasizes the ideal of the presence of God in the things themselves. He writes in his life of Francis: "through God's vestiges imprinted on creation he [Francis] followed his beloved everywhere, making from all things a ladder by which he could climb up and embrace him who is utterly desirable."

That ascent to God is detailed in Bonaventure's most famous work, *The Soul's Journey into God.* The seven chapters of this book are arranged around the theme of a journey. The spiritual life is seen as an ascent through three levels into God. Herein is contained a rich idea, one that static notions of health and sickness give little notice to. Spiritual health is seen not simply as "being saved" or even as "doing good" but as a journey over time, a journey deeper into the mystery of God; a lifelong, indeed an eternity-long progression that involves our whole selves and brings our souls— our truest, most essential selves—to the place where they can participate in the very life of God.

Today there are many who talk similarly about sharing the divine nature. Many who are part of what is loosely called New Age thought have a vivid conception of the progressive nature of the spiritual life and a keen awareness of its tremendous potential. What they often do not have is any sense of the obstacles to reaching those spiritual heights. Put another way, they have no concept of the reality of evil.

Bonaventure lived in an age that would not tolerate such quixotic speculation. His book that speaks of the most sublime ascent of the soul into the very essence of the Godhead begins not with glowing accounts of a beatific vision or upbeat reports of what can be accomplished by the self-actualized person who follows his teaching but with a vision of the cross of Christ. When in the midst of a retreat on Mount La Verna, Bonaventure, like Francis, saw a vision of the crucified Jesus in the form of a six-winged seraph. The six wings Bonaventure took to symbolize the six levels of illumination that the soul passes through on its journey. The message is clear: There is no other path to enlightenment than through the crucified Christ. Like Francis, Bonaventure believed that there was a profound truth to be learned in the acceptance of the reality of suffering. It was not simply to be ignored as some, like Kierkegaard's aesthetic man, might try to do by living his life according to a "hedonistic calculus." Nor could it be avoided by leading a life of detachment, as might be suggested by the Eight-fold Path of Buddhism. Rather it is to be embraced in all its strength, in all its horror. For in that moment of identification with suffering, one ends the hold that evil has. At that instant a momentous act of self-transcendence occurs. You are no longer an isolated individual dealing with the unpleasantness of life. Instead you are part of all of the sufferings of humanity. You are in solidarity with the weak and the poor and the lame, and with all that is broken. Then, and only then, can you know the same power that raised Christ from the dead and be lifted with Him to a new horizon.

So Bonaventure writes:

> I invite the reader to the groans of prayer through Christ crucified, through whose blood we are cleansed from the filth of vice—so that we not believe that reading is sufficient without devotion, investigation without wonder, observation without joy, work without love, understanding without humility, endeavor without divine grace....
>
> To those wishing to give themselves to glorifying, wondering at and even savoring God, I propose the following considerations, suggesting that the mirror presented by the external world is of little or no value unless the mirror of our soul has been cleaned and polished. Therefore, man of God, first exercise yourself in remorse of conscience before you raise your eyes to the rays of Wisdom reflected in its mirrors, lest perhaps from gazing upon these rays you fall into a deeper pit of darkness. (Trans. Ewert Cousins, 1978, p. 56)

With that starting point, Bonaventure presents the three stages of ascent (each with two levels, yielding six, to correspond with the six wings of the seraph). We must first pass through God's vestiges, which are part of the material world. We then enter into our soul, which is God's image. Finally we go beyond that to gazing on the eternal First Principle. Each stage intensifies in brightness, like the day.

The first level, as we have seen, understands the material world as sign and sacrament. We need only add that the perception of beauty in the material things of the world itself becomes a reflection of God. When we perceive beauty in, say, a flower, we

take pleasure in its harmonious symmetry. We get within ourselves a sense, a feeling, an idea about the object that we have
gazed upon. That thing, in our example, that flower, produces
within us a likeness of itself. That likeness for Bonaventure is not
only a reflection of the beautiful flower but also of the eternal
generation of the Word, the Image and the Son, eternally emanating from the Father.

That process by which the Son eternally emanates from the
Father is best understood when Jesus is conceived of as the Eternal
Art of the Father. Art is the work of the artist's hands by which he
brings to life his innermost thoughts and feelings. In Jesus, the
Father expresses all that he can make. The Son contains the ideas,
the patterns, for all things; in him they have an Eternal existence.
The process of the Father begetting the Son as his Eternal Art goes
on continually. As we pray in the Nicene Creed, the Word is "eternally begotten of the Father."

All of creation is sustained in and by the Eternal Art. Every
act of human "creation" is a joint act with the Eternal Art. It is at
this point that the artist in his very work can experience a unity
with God. That unity is a reality brought about in the holy incarnation of Christ. Jesus is the intersection of the human and the
divine in which all that is truly human is exalted and brought into
union with God.

Jesus is the great coincidence of opposites. As Bonaventure
writes in describing the mystical vision of the Eternal Art:

> The mind sees man made to the image of God. For an image
> is an expressed likeness, when our mind contemplates in
> Christ the Son of God, who is the image of God by nature,
> our humanity so wonderfully exalted, so ineffably united,
> when at the same time it sees united the first and the last, the
> highest and the lowest, the circumference and the center, the
> Alpha and the Omega, the caused and the cause, the Creator
> and the creature, that is the book written within and with-
> out, it now reaches something perfect.

The second level involves contemplating God through his image stamped upon our own persons. Seeing God through his vestiges in creation leads us to reenter ourselves. Bonaventure invites us to:

> Enter into yourself, then, and see that your soul loves itself most fervently; that it could not love itself unless it knows itself, or know itself unless it remembered itself, because our intellects grasp only what is present to our memories. From this you can observe, not with the bodily eye, but with the eye of reason, that your soul has a threefold power. Consider, therefore, the operations and relationships of these three powers, and you will be able to see God through yourself as through an image, which is to see through a mirror in an obscure manner.

Here Bonaventure adapts the thought of Augustine of Hippo, who almost a millennium earlier had given the first major statement of image mysticism to the Latin church. Augustine taught that the person in her powers of intellect, memory, and will is an image of the Trinity. The way to ascent to God was to enter into oneself and there encounter God, who is nearer to us than we are to ourselves. In the true self, the self made in the image of God, there is a reflection of the Father, Son, and Holy Spirit.

Bonaventure does not modify this Augustinian tradition of the turn within as the way to ascent to God in any significant way. The memory corresponds to the Father, the intellect to the Son, and the will to the Holy Spirit. By remembrance the memory retains temporal things past. By reception it retains things present and by foresight, things future. But in good Platonic fashion, both Augustine and Bonaventure held that the memory was not only informed from its perception of objects outside the person, but also by receiving and holding within itself forms that cannot enter through the senses: "On that basis," writes Bonaventure, "one can see, they teach, that the memory has an unchangeable light present to itself in which it remembers immutable truths."

The intellect gives us understanding that leads to the truth. The truth is the Son in whom are all knowledge and all wisdom.

The will, which corresponds to the Spirit, gives us the power to desire and to love. We desire that which makes us happy, but in fact only what is best and ultimate can make us happy. Thus the will leads us in our decision making and in our loving to the highest good, God, if lust does not obscure our understanding into confusing an inferior goal for the highest good.

The implications for the artist are evident. When the artist looks for inspiration, he need not look only in the book of the Scriptures and draw material exclusively from the stories and symbols of the Bible. Likewise he need not look only to the book of nature. As valuable as the grand expanse of the earth might be to bring to the artist material for his creations, it does not exhaust the possible resources.

The artist may also look within at the very working of his mind in the memory, understanding, and will and be well served. What he will see there will not be only feelings, thoughts, moods that are of no value or that are peculiar and of no meaning to anyone else. No, for Bonaventure, as for Augustine, those things are reflections of God in the Trinity and, as such, are also meaningful to every other human made in the image and likeness of God.

BIBLIOGRAPHY

Bonaventure: The Soul's Journey into God: The Tree of Life; The Life of St. Francis, trans. Ewert Cousins. The Classics of Western Spirituality. New York/Mahwah, N.J.: Paulist Press, 1978.

Bourgerol, Jacques Guy. *Introduction to the Works of Bonaventure.* Trans.

De Vinck, Jose. Paterson, N.J.: St. Anthony Guild Press, 1964.

Gilson, Etienne. *The Philosophy of St. Bonaventure.* Trans. D. I. Trethowan and F. J. Sheed. London and New York: Sheed and Ward, 1938.

THE SOUL'S JOURNEY INTO GOD[7]

CHAPTER TWO

ON CONTEMPLATING GOD
IN HIS VESTIGES
IN THE SENSE WORLD

11. From the first two stages
in which we are led to behold God
in vestiges,
like the two wings covering the Seraph's feet,
we can gather that all the creatures of the sense world
lead the mind
of the contemplative and wise man
to the eternal God.
For these creatures are
shadows, echoes and pictures
of that first, most powerful, most wise and most perfect
Principle,
of that eternal Source, Light and Fulness,
of that efficient, exemplary and ordering Art.
They are
vestiges, representations, spectacles
proposed to us
and signs divinely given
so that we can see God.
These creatures, I say, are
exemplars

---

7. *Bonaventure: The Soul's Journey into God; The Tree of Life; The Life of St. Francis,* trans. Ewert Cousins, the Classics of Western Spirituality (New York/Mahwah, N.J.: Paulist Press, 1978).

or rather exemplifications
presented to souls still untrained
and immersed in sensible things
so that through sensible things
which they see
they will be carried over to intelligible things
which they do not see
as through signs to what is signified.

12. The creatures of the sense world
signify
the invisible attributes of God,
partly because God is
the origin, exemplar and end
of every creature,
and every effect is
the sign of its cause, the exemplification of its exemplar
and the path to the end, to which it leads:
partly by their own proper representation,
partly from prophetic prefiguration,
partly from angelic operation,
partly from additional institution.
For every creature is by its nature
a kind of effigy and likeness of the eternal Wisdom,
but especially one
which in the book of Scripture
has been elevated through the spirit of prophecy
to prefigure spiritual things;
and more especially, those creatures
in whose likeness God wished to appear
through the ministry of angels;
and most especially, a creature
which God willed to institute
as a symbol
and which has the character

not only of a sign in the general sense
but also of a sacrament.

13. From all this, one can gather that
from the creation of the world
the invisible attributes of God are clearly seen,
being understood
through the things that are made.
And so those who do not wish to heed these things,
and to know, bless and love
God
in all of them
are without excuse;
for they are unwilling to be transported
out of darkness
into the marvelous light of God.
But thanks be to God
through our Lord Jesus Christ,
who *has transported* us
out of darkness
into his marvelous light
when through these lights exteriorly given
we are disposed to reenter
the mirror of our mind
in which divine realities shine forth.

CHAPTER THREE
ON CONTEMPLATING GOD
THROUGH HIS IMAGE
STAMPED UPON OUR NATURAL POWERS

1. The two previous stages, by leading us
into God
through his vestiges,
through which he shines forth

in all creatures,
have led us to the point
of reentering into ourselves, that is,
into our mind,
where the divine image shines forth.
Here it is that, now in the third stage,
we enter into our very selves;
and, as it were, leaving the outer court,
we should strive to see God
through a mirror
in the sanctuary, that is, in the forward area of the tabernacle.
Here the light of truth,
as from a candelabrum,
glows upon the face of our mind,
in which the image of the most blessed Trinity
shines in splendor.
Enter into yourself, then, and see
that your soul loves itself most fervently;
that it could not love itself
unless it knew itself,
nor know itself
unless it remembered itself,
because our intellects grasp only what is present to our memory.
From this you can observe,
not with the bodily eye, but with the eye of reason,
that your soul has a threefold power.
Consider, therefore,
the operations and relationships of these three powers,
and you will be able to see God
through yourself as through an image,
which is to see *through a mirror in an obscure manner.*

2. The function of memory is to retain and represent not only
present, corporeal and temporal things but also successive, simple and
eternal things. For the memory retains the past by remembrance, the

present by reception and the future by foresight. It retains also simple things, such as the principles of continuous and discrete quantities like the point, the instant and the unit. Without these it is impossible to remember or to think of things which originate from them. The memory also retains the principles and axioms of the sciences, as everlasting truths held everlastingly. For while using reason, one can never so completely forget these principles that he would fail to approve and assent to them once they are heard, not as if he perceives them anew, but rather as if he recognizes them as innate and familiar. This is clearly shown when we propose to someone the following: "On any matter, one must either affirm or deny," or "Every whole is greater than its part," or any other axiom which cannot be contradicted "by our inner reason."

In its first activity, therefore—the actual retention of all temporal things, past, present and future—the memory is an image of eternity, whose indivisible presence extends to all times. From its second activity, it is evident that memory is informed not only from outside by sensible images, but also from above by receiving and holding within itself simple forms which cannot enter through the doors of the senses by means of sensible images. From the third activity, we hold that the memory has an unchangeable light present to itself in which it remembers immutable truths. And so from the activities of the memory, we see that the soul itself is an image of God and a likeness so present to itself and having God so present that the soul actually grasps him and potentially "is capable of possessing him and of being a partaker in him."

3. The function of the intellective faculty consists in understanding the meaning of terms, propositions and inferences. Now, the intellect grasps the meaning of terms when it comprehends in a definition what a thing is. But definitions are constructed by using more universal terms; and these are defined by more universal terms until we come to the highest and most universal. Consequently, unless these latter are known, the less universal cannot be grasped in a definition. Unless we know what being per se is, we cannot fully know the definition of any particular substance. We

cannot know being per se unless we also know its properties, which are: one, true, good. Now, being can be considered as incomplete or complete, as imperfect or perfect, as being in potency or being in act, qualified being or unqualified being, partial being or total being, transient being or permanent being, being through another or being through itself, being mixed with nonbeing or pure being, dependent being or absolute being, posterior being or prior being, changeable being or unchangeable being, simple being or composite being. Since privations and defects can in no way be known except through something positive, our intellect does not come to the point of understanding any created being by a full analysis unless it is aided by a knowledge of the Being which is most pure, most actual, most complete and absolute, which is unqualified and Eternal Being, in which are the principles of all things in their purity. How could the intellect know that a particular being is defective and incomplete if it had no knowledge of the Being which is free from all defect? The same holds true for the other properties previously mentioned.

The intellect can be said truly to comprehend the meaning of propositions when it knows with certitude that they are true. To know this is really to know because the intellect cannot be deceived in this kind of comprehension. For it knows that this truth cannot be otherwise; therefore, it knows that this truth is unchangeable. But since our mind itself is changeable, it can see such a truth shining forth unchangingly only by means of some light which shines in an absolutely unchangeable way; and it is impossible for this light to be a changeable creature. Therefore our intellect knows in that Light *which enlightens every man coming into this world,* which is *the true Light* and the *Word* who *was in the beginning with God* (John 1:9, 1).

Our intellect truly grasps the meaning of an inference when it sees that the conclusion follows necessarily from the premises. It sees this not only in necessary but also in contingent terms such as the following: If a man is running, the man is moving. Our intellect perceives this necessary relationship not only in existing things, but also in nonexisting things. For if a man actually exists, it follows that if he is running, he is moving; the same conclusion follows even if he does not exist. The necessity, therefore, of this inference does not come from the existence of the thing in matter since it is contingent; nor from the existence of the thing in the soul because that would be a fiction if the thing did not exist in reality. Therefore the necessity of such an inference comes from its exemplarity in the Eternal Art, according to which things are mutually oriented and related to one another because they are represented in the Eternal Art. As Augustine says in *On the True Religion:* The light of everyone who reasons truly is enkindled by that Truth which he also strives to reach. From this it is obvious that our intellect is joined to Eternal Truth itself since it can grasp no truth with certitude if it is not taught by this Truth. You can see, therefore, through yourself the Truth which teaches you, if your desires and sensory images do not hinder you and interpose themselves like clouds between you and the rays of Truth.

4.   The function of the power of choice is found in deliberation, judgment and desire. Deliberation consists in inquiring which is better, this or that. But *better* has meaning only in terms of its proximity to *best;* and this proximity is in terms of greater resemblance. No one, therefore, knows whether this is better than that unless he knows that it bears a greater resemblance to the best. No one knows that something bears a greater resemblance to another unless he knows the other. For I do not know that a certain man resembles Peter unless I know Peter or have some acquaintance with him. Therefore, the notion of the highest good is necessarily imprinted in everyone who deliberates.

A judgment of certitude on matters of deliberation is made according to some law. But no one judges with certitude according to law unless he is certain that the law is right and that he should not judge the law itself. But our mind judges about itself. Since, then, it cannot judge about the law through which it judges, that law is higher than our mind; and our mind judges by means of that law insofar as it is imprinted on our mind. But nothing is higher than the human mind except him alone who made it. Therefore in judging, our deliberative power touches the divine laws if it reaches a solution by a full analysis.

Now desire tends principally toward what moves it most, but what moves it most is what is loved most, and what is loved most is happiness. But happiness is had only in terms of the best and ultimate end. Therefore human desire seeks nothing except the highest good or what leads to or has some likeness to it. So great is the power of the highest good that nothing can be loved by a creature except out of a desire for it. Creatures, when they take the image and copy for the Truth, are deceived and in error.

See, therefore, how close the soul is to God, and how, in their operations, the memory leads to eternity, the understanding to truth and the power of choice to the highest good.

5. These powers lead us to the most blessed Trinity itself in view of their order, origin and interrelatedness. From memory, intelligence comes forth as its offspring, since we understand when a likeness which is in the memory leaps into the eye of the intellect in the form of a word. From memory and intelligence love is breathed forth as their mutual bond. These three—the generating mind, the word and love—are in the soul as memory, understanding and will, which are consubstantial, coequal and coeval, and interpenetrate each other. If, then, God is a perfect spirit, he has memory, understanding and will; and he has the Word generated and Love breathed forth, which are necessarily distinct since one is produced by the other—not in the order of essence, not in the order of accident, therefore in the order of persons.

When, therefore, the soul considers itself, it rises through itself as through a mirror to behold the blessed Trinity of the Father, the Word and Love: three persons, coeternal, coequal and consubstantial. Thus each one dwells in each of the others; nevertheless one is not the other but the three are one God.

6. When the soul considers its Triune Principle through the trinity of its powers, by which it is an image of God, it is aided by the lights of the sciences which perfect and inform it and represent

the most blessed Trinity in a threefold way. For all philosophy is either natural or rational or moral. The first deals with the cause of being and therefore leads to the power of the Father; the second deals with the basis of understanding and therefore leads to the wisdom of the Word; the third deals with the order of living and therefore leads to the goodness of the Holy Spirit.

Again, the first, natural philosophy, is divided into metaphysics, mathematics and physics. The first deals with the essences of things; the second with numbers and figures; and the third with natures, powers and diffusive operations. Therefore the first leads to the First Principle, the Father; the second to his Image, the Son; and the third to the gift of the Holy Spirit.

The second, rational philosophy, is divided into grammar, which makes men able to express themselves; logic, which makes them skillful in arguing; and rhetoric, which makes them capable of persuading and moving others. This likewise suggests the mystery of the most blessed Trinity.

The third, moral philosophy, is divided into individual, domestic and political. The first suggests the unbegottenness of the First Principle; the second, the relatedness of the Son; and the third, the liberality of the Holy Spirit.

> 7. All these sciences have certain and infallible rules,
> like rays of light shining down upon our mind
> from the eternal law.
> And thus our mind, illumined and flooded
> by such brilliance,
> unless it is blind,
> can be led through itself
> to contemplate that Eternal Light.
> The radiation and contemplation
> of this Light
> lifts up the wise in wonder;
> and on the contrary
> it leads to confusion the fools

who do not believe so that they may understand.
Thus this prophecy is fulfilled:
You enlighten wonderfully
from the eternal hills;
all the foolish of heart
were troubled.

★   ★   ★

CHAPTER SEVEN
ON
SPIRITUAL AND MYSTICAL ECSTASY
IN WHICH REST IS GIVEN TO OUR
INTELLECT
WHEN THROUGH ECSTASY OUR
AFFECTION
PASSES OVER ENTIRELY TO GOD

1. We have, therefore, passed through
these six considerations.
They are like
the six steps of the true Solomon's throne,
by which we arrive
at peace,
where the true man of peace
rests in a peaceful mind
as in the interior Jerusalem.

They are also like
the six wings of the Seraph
by which the mind of the true contemplative
can be borne aloft,
filled with the illumination of heavenly wisdom.

They are also like the first six days,
in which the mind has been trained so that it may reach
the sabbath of rest.

After our mind has beheld God
outside itself
through his vestiges and in his vestiges,
within itself
through his image and in his image,
and above itself
through the similitude of the divine Light shining above us
and in the Light itself,
insofar as this is possible in our state as wayfarers
and through the exercise of our mind,
when finally in the sixth stage
our mind reaches that point
where it contemplates
in the First and Supreme Principle
and in the *mediator of God and men,*
Jesus Christ,
those things whose likenesses can in no way be found
in creatures
and which surpass all penetration
by the human intellect,
it now remains for our mind,
by contemplating these things,
to transcend and pass over not only this sense world
but even itself.
In this passing over,
Christ is the *way and the door;*
Christ is the ladder and the vehicle,
like the Mercy Seat placed above the ark of God
and the *mystery hidden from eternity.*

2. Whoever turns his face fully to the Mercy Seat
and with faith, hope and love,
devotion, admiration, exultation,
appreciation, praise and joy
beholds him hanging upon the cross,

such a one makes the Pasch, that is, the passover,
with Christ.
By the staff of the cross
he passes over the Red Sea,
going from Egypt into the desert,
where he will taste the *hidden manna;*
and with Christ
he rests in the tomb,
as if dead to the outer world,
but experiencing,
as far as is possible in this wayfarer's state,
what was said on the cross
to the thief who adhered to Christ;
Today you shall be with me in paradise.

3. This was shown also
to blessed Francis,
when in ecstatic contemplation
on the height of the mountain—
where I thought out these things I have written—
there appeared to him
a six-winged Seraph fastened to a cross,
as I and several others heard
in that very place
from his companion who was with him then.
There he passed over into God in ecstatic contemplation
and became an example of perfect contemplation
as he had previously been of action,
like another Jacob and Israel,
so that through him,
more by example than by word,
God might invite all truly spiritual men
to this kind of passing over
and spiritual ecstasy.

4. In this passing over,
if it is to be perfect,
all intellectual activities must be left behind
and the height of our affection
must be totally transferred and transformed
into God.
This, however, is mystical and most secret,
which *no one knows*
except him who receives it,
no one receives
except him who desires it,
and no one desires except him
who is inflamed in his very marrow by the fire of the Holy Spirit
whom Christ sent into the world.
And therefore the Apostle says that
this mystical wisdom is revealed
by the Holy Spirit.

5. Since, therefore, in this regard
nature can do nothing
and effort can do but little,
little importance should be given to inquiry,
but much to unction;
little importance should be given to the tongue,
but much to inner joy;
little importance should be given to words and to writing,
but all to the gift of God,
that is, the Holy Spirit;
little or no importance should be given to creation,
but all to the creative essence,
the Father, Son and Holy Spirit,
saying with Dionysius
to God the Trinity:
"Trinity,
superessential, superdivine and supereminent

overseer of the divine wisdom of Christians,
direct us into
superunknown, superluminous and most sublime
summit
of mystical communication.
There
new, absolute and unchangeable mysteries of theology
are hidden
in the superluminous darkness
of a silence
teaching secretly in the utmost obscurity
which is supermanifest—
a darkness which is super-resplendent
and in which everything shines forth
and which fills to overflowing
invisible intellects
with the splendors of invisible goods
that surpass all good."
This is said to God.
But to the friend to whom these words were written,
let us say with Dionysius:
"But you, my friend,
concerning mystical visions,
with your journey more firmly determined,
leave behind
your senses and intellectual activities,
sensible and invisible things,
all nonbeing and being;
and in this state of unknowing
be restored,
insofar as is possible,
to unity with him
who is above all essence and knowledge.
For transcending yourself and all things,
by the immeasurable and absolute ecstasy of a pure mind,

leaving behind all things
and freed from all things,
you will ascend
to the superessential ray
of the divine darkness."

6. But if you wish to know how these things come about,
ask grace not instruction,
desire not understanding,
the groaning of prayer not diligent reading,
the Spouse not the teacher,
God not man,
darkness not clarity,
not light but the fire
that totally inflames and carries us into God
by ecstatic unctions and burning affections.
This fire is God,
and *his furnace is in Jerusalem;*
and Christ enkindles it
in the heat of his burning passion,
which only he truly perceives who says:
My soul chooses hanging and my bones death.
Whoever loves this death
can see God
because it is true beyond doubt that
man will not see me and live.
Let us, then, die
and enter into the darkness;
let us impose silence
upon our cares, our desires and our imaginings.
With Christ crucified
let us pass *out of this world to the Father*
so that when the Father is shown to us,
we may say with Philip:
It is enough for us.

Let us hear with Paul:
My grace is sufficient for you.
Let us rejoice with David saying:
My flesh and my heart have grown faint;
You are the God of my heart,
and the God that is my portion forever.
Blessed be the Lord forever
and all the people will say:
Let it be; let it be.
Amen.

HERE ENDS THE SOUL'S JOURNEY INTO GOD.